Vernon Blackwood

DIAL 911

DIAL 911

Peaceful Christians and Urban Violence

Dave Jackson

Introduction by
Howard Zehr, Jr.

HERALD PRESS
Scottdale, Pennsylvania
Kitchener, Ontario
1981

Library of Congress Cataloging in Publication Data

Jackson, Dave.
    Dial 911.

    1. Reba Place Fellowship (Evanston, Ill.) 2. Violence—Moral and
religious aspects. 3. Crime and criminals—Illinois—Evanston.
I. Title. II. Title: Peaceful Christians and urban violence.
BV4407.8.J3   261.8'33   81-2541
ISBN 0-8361-1952-5 (pbk.)   AACR2

Scripture quotations from the Revised Standard Version of the Bible, copyrighted
1946, 1952, © 1971, 1973.

DIAL 911: *Peaceful Christians and Urban Violence*
Copyright © 1981 by Herald Press, Scottdale, Pa. 15683
    Published simultaneously in Canada by Herald Press,
    Kitchener, Ont. N2G 4M5
Library of Congress Catalog Card Number: 81-2541
International Standard Book Number: 0-8361-1952-5
Printed in the United States of America
Design: Alice B. Shelter/Cover: James Converse

81 82 83 84 85 86 10 9 8 7 6 5 4 3 2 1

Also by Dave Jackson:

Living Together in a World Falling Apart
    (with Neta Jackson)
Coming Together

Contents

Introduction

Dial 911 recounts Reba Place Fellowship's recent experiences with crime in Evanston, Illinois, along with observations and reflections. It is engrossing because much of it is in story form. It is encouraging because of the variety of responses which are reflected, but also because of the openness, willingness to question, and freedom to admit error which is evident.

Should we call the police? Reba Place's answer is no, and yes. In certain circumstances they have been moved to work with the police; in other cases, they have not.

If we choose to summon the police, Jackson says we must not evade our responsibility for what happens thereafter. What responsibility do we have for the offender? Is there a difference in appropriate responses, depending on whether we are victimized or someone else is the victim? Are there situations in which we must physically help to restrain an offender? Is force ever justified? Should we feel guilty about the emotions of anger and invasion that we may feel as a victim? These are a few of the questions *Dial 911* addresses.

Often we assume the answers without questioning. For example, who stops to think before calling the police whether this is an appropriate response for the people of God? Perhaps it is appropriate, but we must ask the question. Christians who see themselves as called to be different from the world cannot, without examination, simply accept the world's normal response.

Jackson does not offer pat answers. He comments on basic principles which are central to our faith. But he also recognizes that responses must vary depending upon circumstances and—and this is most important—upon the leading of the Spirit.

Dial 911 is important because it contains testimonies, provides some general guidelines, but especially because it urges us to question and to be open to God's will.

I hope *Dial 911* is widely read and that it helps Christians in many communities increase their concern both for victims and for offenders.

Howard Zehr, Jr.
Elkhart, Indiana

Howard Zehr, Jr., is director of the Victim-Offender Reconciliation Program of Elkhart (Ind.) County's chapter of PACT, Inc. (Prisoner and Community Together). He is also director of the Office of Criminal Justice for Mennonite Central Committee (MCC) in the United States.

Author's Preface

What would you do if someone broke into your home and began to carry out your possessions?

- Reach for a gun?
- Turn the other cheek?
- Dial 911 to call the police?

We've not found the answer to crime and violence to be that simple. I am a member of Reba Place Fellowship, an intentional church community which has been in Evanston on Chicago's North Side for the past 23 years. Murders, rapes, and armed robberies have increased several fold in that time. For 1979, Evanston's per capita burglary rate was double that reported in Chicago. And our "poorer," more congested part of the city experienced more than its share of those statistics.

But what should we do?

One approach would be to arm ourselves with weapons, guard dogs, the most sophisticated electronic alarm systems, maybe even join with neighbors to hire a private security company to patrol our streets. But then we'd need to learn how to shoot, practice martial arts, train our guard dogs, set the alarms, and double bolt the door. That's one approach, and with today's rising crime rate many people have resorted to it. But it's not a pleasant solution to the problem. When you take on the job of defending yourself, you don't really sleep easier. You're tense, preoccupied with the task, paranoid that the next criminal will have a better weapon, a higher degree in karate, or enough brains to circumvent the most advanced burglar alarm. It's like trying to be the high school tough guy. Sooner or later you'll meet your match, and in the meantime life is charged with anxiety.

Another response would be to promote the role of the police, encouraging arrests and swift convictions which send criminals to prison at every opportunity. But that approach has its problems too. The major riots and carnage at the Attica and Santa Fe prisons are grisly reminders of the failure of America's prison system to accomplish its mission ... by any standard. For those who think that prisons should reform criminals, records show little hope for success. We've nearly come to accept prisons as graduate schools for criminals, toughening and educating them for more serious crimes upon release. For those who hope that the threat of incarceration will deter crime, the rates seem unaffected by the likelihood of serving time. Even those who want vengeance are unsatisfied because they erroneously think prisons coddle criminals. (Nonetheless, they would probably cringe from sentencing a person to the kind of punishment which too often *is* delivered in prison—gang rapes, beatings, and murder.)

But we do not want vengeance. We are Christians who feel called to stand against the violent treatment of any person. Prisons, as they exist today, seem like a hopeless solution to crime. So calling the police and starting a process which would send a person to prison is seldom satisfactory. And even the threat of death which the policeman's gun introduces into a situation is disturbing because we cannot easily wash our hands of what he might do when we turn the situation over to him. We still feel some responsibility—a responsibility not to harm a fellow human or, in the more radical words of Jesus, "Do not resist one who is evil."

How do we obey that? It seems like an impossible ideal, but in our intentional church community in Evanston we have tried. We have tried to find alternatives to the more violent and hopeless approaches to crime as we've experienced it. And we've experienced a lot! Most of the stories in this book happened during the past five years, to the people in a relatively small church of about 300, all living in a five-block area of our city. And even these stories are only a sample of the many other crimes which have happened to us and others in our neighborhood during that time.

We still don't know what to do in the sense of having *the answer,* but we've developed a few guidelines—some helpful distinctions between kinds of crime and kinds of criminals and the potential for justice in various situations. We've discovered some creative and effective deterrents to crime which don't threaten anyone's life, and we've seen what an important role our attitudes play in resolving conflicts and promoting peace in our neighborhood.

Some of our experiences reflect creative faithfulness. In some we must confess failure. Still others display God's intervention. But they all are valuable because they touch reality and move beyond theory.

Dave Jackson
Evanston, Illinois

DIAL 911

1
Time Goes By

The afternoon's quiet was interrupted only by the intermittent clatter of my old typewriter. The yellow and brown leaves from the large elm trees on our street made no noise as they drifted to the ground. In my usual way, I'd get up and pace around my basement office, trying to think of how to put the next few words together.

Ralph Lind, who along with his wife and several other folks lived in our extended family household, the Branch, had just returned from his classes for the day at the University of Illinois' Circle Campus. He was making a big sandwich in the kitchen when Jennifer Miller came running in.

"Quick. There's something going on at our house that's not right. There's a strange person in there."

Her urgency communicated more than her words. Ralph called me, and we ran out the front door and down the street to the next Fellowship house on the block—four doors west.

Ralph went around to the back door as I ran up the front steps. We're truly like family in the Fellowship, so I barged right in, through the vestibule and up to the strange woman standing in the open doorway of the dining room.

"What's going on here?"

She whirled around to face me.

She was young, tall, and strongly built. She wore tight Levis, a Levi jacket, tall boots, and dark glasses that faded to almost clear at the bottom. Her hair was tied up under a brown beret, and in her clenched fist just before my face she held a ten-inch knife.

As I recall what happened, it is like studying the individual frames of a movie film. The action was stopped, the time was extended, and I thought about far more than should fit into a person's mind in one moment.

Behind her was the dining room table. At the corner nearest me sat old Ruth Beckstrom, 85, with a rag wrapped around a badly bleeding hand. To the left was Robin Wood, sitting up straight and strangely immobile. Across the table sat Vicki Lichti with her two-year-old Toby on her lap. In the corner, at the right end of the table was baby Ethan's bassinet. Vicki had given birth to him less than two weeks before. In the adjoining room two other children played.

Were there other intruders in the house looting rooms while this one stood guard? I wondered. *Would they have weapons, possibly guns? How do I respond nonviolently with the point of a knife inches from my throat?*

I believe the Lord spoke to me then. "Grab her wrist. You will not be hurt, and you will not have to hurt her."

I grabbed and caught a solid grip. My action was so fast that the woman was too surprised to respond or she was divinely weakened, because I was able to move the knife away from my throat with little resistance.

"Get Ralph," I said. "He's coming in the back." But no one around the table moved. *Did someone I couldn't see have a gun pointed toward them?*

The woman was reaching for the knife with her other

hand. Her resistance increased. The Lord spoke again. "Get her out of the doorway. The people behind her are too close. If you slipped, they could get hurt."

I pulled, put out my leg, and tripped her as she came across. She went down, and I pinned her to the floor. We were safe for the moment. She was strong, but she wouldn't get free easily, even though I still had to watch out for the knife.

"Ralph," I yelled, "hurry, I need you." *Where was he? Had he met with somebody else?* And then he was there, prying the knife from the woman's hand.

"What's your name?" I said.

"Elizabeth." °

"What were you doing?"

"I didn't do anything. I just needed some money. Just get off me."

"Should we call the police?" someone asked.

"Don't call the police, man! I didn't do anything. I'll give her her rings back. I swear. Just let me go."

"Shut up, and let me think," I said.

Here we were, back to that question. What should we do? The crisis was over. What was done was done. How would Jesus respond? If we gave her some money and turned her loose maybe she'd be so shocked that she'd want to know Jesus. Then again, maybe she'd rob someone else next week and even kill someone in the process.

At that moment a policeman walked in the door. Jennifer had dialed 911 from the Branch after getting Ralph and me. A squad car was in the area and responded in a matter of moments.

°Within this book, when only the first name of a person is introduced, it is not the person's real name.

My first thought was to wonder how I was going to explain the scene to the policeman. There I was pinning a woman to the floor after an obvious fracas. It wasn't my house, and I didn't really know what had happened. Had she robbed somebody? Had she only tried to rob somebody? And how had old Ruth's hand been cut? The knife was on the floor just a few feet away. What would happen if the woman quick-talked the cops by saying that I was the attacker?

It was an irrational stream of worries. Soon other policemen arrived and the sergeant quickly figured out what was happening.

"Are you going to press charges?" he asked.

"Yes," I answered. I figured that we could say yes in that moment and buy some time for a more careful decision. Later, if we wanted, we could drop the charges.

The policeman told the woman that she was under arrest. The moment that they touched her to put on handcuffs, she began fighting with a fury unlike anything she had done with me. She was screaming and yelling, and the three policemen had a real handful trying to control her. They did get the handcuffs on her, but by the time they got her down to the station, she had twisted them up like pretzels.

∘ ∘ ∘

The whole ordeal had begun nearly an hour earlier when Vicki had answered her front door to find a woman in her mid-twenties asking if there was a room she could rent. When Vicki said, "No," the woman first claimed to be selling Avon and then insurance. When that did not gain her entrance, she started inching her way in, saying that she wanted to speak confidentially to Vicki about the old woman sitting on the porch, Ruth Beckstrom.

Once inside, she drew a knife from her boot. The tip of the knife was broken off, but the blade was still about ten inches long. She demanded that Vicki give her money, rings, and all other valuables. Vicki surrendered her rings but was only able to turn up about $3 in change. That was unsatisfactory to Elizabeth. So she sent Vicki out to get Ruth while she threatened Vicki's two-year-old son, Toby.

Shortly after Vicki returned with Ruth, Robin Wood came up the walk with her eighteen-month-old Jeremy. Robin saw what was happening as she started to come in and tried to flee, but Elizabeth ran out and pulled her in. Meanwhile Ruth tried to escape up to her room where she could lock herself in. However, her age prevented her from moving very fast, and Elizabeth, forcing the others to accompany her, followed Ruth and demanded her money. When Ruth refused to surrender more than $20, Elizabeth slashed wildly at her and severely cut her hand. Then Ruth gave her the rest of her money, which totaled more than $200 because of a recently cashed Social Security check.

Elizabeth then brought everyone downstairs and began to tie them up, starting with Robin. (That's why when I came in they seemed to be sitting so stiffly in their chairs. Their hands were tied to the chairs behind their backs where I couldn't see them.) During this procedure, Elizabeth expressed regret that she had cut Ruth's hand. She kept saying that she hadn't meant to do it and soon found an old dish towel to wrap around the wound to try to stop the bleeding. Elizabeth said that she was tying them loosely enough that they could get free in a while after she left. She mentioned that she too had kids and wouldn't hurt Vicki's and Robin's children.

During this entire time Ethan remained sound asleep in his bassinet with a thin blanket over him. It didn't appear as though Elizabeth ever noticed him.

Before Elizabeth had tied everyone up with extension cords, Jennifer Miller came quietly in the door. She'd gotten off early from her work that day. She overheard Elizabeth telling them not to call the police. Vicki was able to signal to her with her head to leave before Elizabeth heard or saw her. That's when Jennifer ran down to the Branch to get help from Ralph and me and phone the police.

∘ ∘ ∘

After the police left with Elizabeth, I accompanied Ruth in the ambulance to the hospital emergency room where she received 14 stitches in her hand. During the next few days we spent a lot of time talking with the children and everyone else involved, trying to process the trauma of the whole experience.

It turned out that Elizabeth fit the description of a woman who had robbed and cut a man's arm the night before near the local train stop. She was a dope addict supporting a $70-a-day habit. She had been in trouble several times before and had gone through various drug treatment programs without success.

We tried to pray and think about whether we should follow through with pressing charges. We called a Christian rehabilitation program for women in Chicago to see if they would be willing to take Elizabeth if we could arrange for her release into their custody. They were not prepared to take anyone with a record as serious as hers.

And then, before we had come to any decision, we heard that at the arraignment Elizabeth had pleaded guilty to armed robbery and assault with a deadly weapon. The judge sentenced her on the spot, and she had been shipped immediately downstate to Illinois' prison for women at

Dwight, Illinois. She would begin serving a four-to-ten-year sentence, with the first possible parole in about eighteen months.

My one brief word, "Yes," when the policeman asked me if we would press charges had resulted in putting a needy mother of two children in prison for a long time. I felt the weight that judges must bear when their word so seriously affects the lives of individuals. I don't think I really felt guilt; I just felt the serious weight of what I had said. I thought about the hundreds of places I had gone over the last eighteen months, the thousands of things I had chosen to do with the time and freedom that were mine. Eighteen months is a long time. What would happen to her children? Would she be safe in prison? Would she come out better equipped to cope with life?

On the other hand, she was a dangerous woman, a real threat to the safety of other people. There is no way that a person like her could avoid a life of violent crime to support a $70-a-day habit. It was an illusion to imagine that she had given anything worthwhile to her children for a long time. They had lost the care of a loving mother long before she went to prison. And on top of that we didn't have any realistic alternative to offer her, even if we had had the chance.

Still, as the months went by, I often thought about Elizabeth. Sometimes I'd worry that when she got out she'd come back for revenge, or that she'd send some accomplice to do the job for her. But usually I worried more about how she was doing, what was happening to her. And I thought about the consequences of my one word.

The Lord gave Robin Wood courage to write to Elizabeth. Several months passed with no response. Finally, Robin received an answer.

The letter was a little awkward, but sincere. Elizabeth apologized for what she had done. She said that she was doing okay. In fact, she said that she was in better emotional and physical health than she had been in years.

Then I wrote to Elizabeth also and told her who I was. I acknowledged that it felt strange to write to her because I didn't know whether she loathed me or not. Her answer was prompt and warm. Again it contained a deep apology and an assurance that she was doing well.

Robin and I have corresponded with Elizabeth several times since then, and just recently we went down to visit her, fourteen months after the robbery.

The prison is out in the flat, ice-covered Illinois countryside. Only a few trees around the gatehouse challenge the starkness of the high stone walls with their rolls of barbed concertina wire on the top. We waited in the entry room until the guard could come out and search us and fill out the forms. I noticed on Elizabeth's card that during her whole time there she had had only one other visitor. Later I learned that it was her sister, who since had moved to another part of the country.

In the visiting room we sat for more than a half hour waiting for a guard to go get Elizabeth. It turned out that Elizabeth was in solitary confinement, unfree to respond to a call on the intercom like some of the more trusted prisoners.

While we were waiting, several of the guards strolled through. The building was the central administration facility, and buzzed with a lot of activity. There seemed to be three kinds of guards. Several were young girls, petite and pretty. They might have been students in some university program. Then there were a number of male guards. But the other female guards surprised me. They were large, muscular, mid-fortyish, with short, bleached hair, deep gravelly voices, and leathery skin. In their tailored green uniforms they could have been actors in a movie about a Nazi prisoner of war camp. They were so stereotypic that I couldn't believe they were real. I talked with one for quite awhile and she seemed nice enough—it was just a job to her—but the appearance was chilling.

Finally, Elizabeth came in. Even though we had only seen each other for a few brief minutes more than a year before, I would have recognized her anywhere. She looked good, healthy, with long dark straight hair. They searched her, and then allowed us to talk for more than two hours.

She told a strange story. She said that she had arrived in prison with a chip on her shoulder, ready to fight with anybody, and sure that her life would be in danger. Withdrawal from drugs had been more than she could take. When the chance came, she and another woman escaped over the wall. In the course of the escape, a guard was beaten repeatedly and severely around the head with a steel bar. He nearly died.

Once over the wall, Elizabeth had no idea where to go. It was the middle of winter with a lot of snow on the ground. Wearing tennis shoes and a thin sweater, she eluded the search teams for seven hours by huddling in snowdrifts when they came by with their searchlights. When they caught her she was only three miles from the prison.

Elizabeth says she took no part in the beating, that it was the work of her partner. But the prison authorities thought otherwise. At the trial they blamed her for the beating. As a result, she has been resentenced and is now serving a maximum of 40 years with no possible parole until after ten years. Ever since the escape she has been held in solitary confinement—allowed two showers and one hour of TV alone per week.

Elizabeth says that after the trial for her escape, she discovered that the prison had taken depositions from ten other inmates that had seen the beating and the escape. All but one said that she did not do the beating. Elizabeth hopes that she can secure a retrial on grounds of suppression of evidence.

At times her isolation seems intolerable to her, but she is personally sure that it has benefited her in many ways. "Ironically, it took this time alone to make me realize that I was headed for destruction. I haven't been as aware and confident as I am now in many, many years. My goal is to become better, not bitter."

Sometimes we just sat and looked at each other for a long time. "Do you feel uncomfortable talking to me?" she asked.

"No, not uncomfortable. I don't really know what to talk about, but I don't feel nervous."

"I was kind of scared to come out when I heard you were here. I didn't know what it would be like." She sat quietly for a while. "You know, whenever I've had a chance to talk to people, even the guards, I've told them about the letters you two have written me. Nobody can believe it. They've never heard of anything like that.

"How's the old lady's hand?" she asked. "You know, I never meant to hurt her." We told her that Ruth was getting along okay, and physically she is. She has full use of her hand again. But emotionally she still lives with fear after the trauma.

"I can remember most of what happened when I stuck you guys up, but I was so smashed out of my head that I can't put together the sequence very well. How did it all happen?"

We reviewed the whole event, all three of us adding some of the details that we remembered most vividly.

"Were you scared?" she asked.

"You bet I was scared," answered Robin. "I didn't know what you were going to do."

"I wouldn't have hurt your kids, you know. You weren't afraid of that, were you?"

"I didn't know what you'd do."

We sat quietly for a long time. Looking at her, I tried to imagine her solitary prison life from day to day. She has a radio and she reads a lot. Being in isolation, she doesn't work in the prison industry. She's just doing time.

"Boy, if I'd known who you people were, I wouldn't have gone into your house."

"Why is that?"

"I was raised in a strict Pentecostal church right there in Evanston. We weren't allowed to do anything—couldn't wear pants, couldn't cut our hair, couldn't do anything. Just before high school graduation, I quit. I couldn't take it any more. Since then I've done everything except kill somebody. But God and the Bible mean something to me. I'm coming back to that more and more. I read the Bible almost every day—things go better when I do. If I'd known you were church people, I wouldn't have come into your house."

"Well, maybe it's better that you did."

"Yeah, maybe."

We talked about the Lord for quite awhile. We asked if there are any church services in the prison. There are, but because of her isolation, she can't attend. She asked to see a chaplain once and even requested that he pray for her. But he said she ought to pray for herself. That was back when she was still so hostile. We asked if she wanted us to pray with her. She thought for a moment and then said no. There were a lot of other people in the visiting room.

"We do pray for you, though."

"Yeah. Thanks. I can tell."

"Are your kids okay?"

"Yeah. They're with my man's family. He's in Pontiac Prison. But the kids are in about the best place they could be."

"Is there anything we could do for you?"

Why was I asking that question? What could I possibly do for Elizabeth? Maybe I did feel guilty. Maybe my visit was just to see that she was okay so that I could live with the thought of where she was. Did I want her to be as reformed as she appeared? Or would it have been easier for me to imagine a "toughened criminal," kept behind bars for the protection and welfare of society and in payment for her evil?

"You could mail this letter for me," she answered. "It's to the Prison Advocacy. Maybe somebody there can help me get out of isolation. Illinois has a law that says that they can't keep you in isolation more than a year. It's been 14 months now for me. The woman that went over the wall with me got out in seven."

"Is there anybody we could contact to help reduce your time?"

"No, there's no chance of that unless I can get a new trial."

"But ten years is so much time."

"Ten years is only my first chance for parole. The board usually turns you down once or twice as a matter of course."

"That sounds like forever," Robin said.

"Well, it's not too bad. I'm already working on my second year."

We'd already said we had to go two or three times. Finally, we stood. "Can we give you a hug?"

She hesitated only a moment. "Yeah."

We turned and the guard let us out of the bar-covered door.

From down the corridor we looked back. Elizabeth was waving from the window. We went out to our cold car and drove down the icy road two hours to Chicago and then up to Evanston.

Time goes by. Elizabeth did her deeds, and I had said my word. We both live with those facts. Of course, somebody else might have agreed to press charges. And they probably would have. There's no chance that Elizabeth could have turned around on her own. But . . . well, in ten years my son will be a man and my daughter will be a young woman. The Lord willing, I will have traveled tens of thousands of miles, celebrated one joyous Christmas after another, and I will have spent much of the prime of my life. The whole world will have changed in ten years.

But for Elizabeth, time goes by . . . and is gone.

2
Victim/Offender Reconciliation

When Fern Nisly opened the front door, the two young black men walked right in without an invitation. She didn't know them, and on the warm Thursday afternoon in late July, no one else was at home. Even the kids were out in the backyard playing.

"Hey, wait a minute. What do you want?" said Fern.

"We're looking for Jack," said the one who was over six feet tall.

"Well, he doesn't live here. He hasn't lived here for a long time."

"Yes he does. We're going upstairs to look for him."

"He doesn't live here. You'll have to leave now," and as short as she is, Fern began pushing one of them toward the door.

"Get your hands off me, woman, and don't give me any lip. We know he's here." They both turned and started up the stairs.

"No, he doesn't live here. He moved. He lives over on Seward Street."

"All right," the tall one said. "Let's get out of here." And they left.

Fern shut the door and stood there shaking for a moment before she went to the back door and called in the kids. In an attempt to return the afternoon to normal, she had the three children go into the living room to try on some new shoes to be sure that they really fit properly. Penny, their nine-year-old foster daughter, had a blister on her heel. So Fern sent her to the bathroom near the back of the house to get a Band-Aid.

"Fern," called Penny as she came running back. "What's that big black guy doing in our bathroom?"

"I don't know."

"Well, there's somebody in there!"

Fern hesitated. Was this one of the men she had just pushed out the front door? If so, what did they want? Why were they so persistent? Should she confront them again, or should she get the kids out of the house and go for help?

On the other hand she didn't want to alarm the children unnecessarily. Penny, herself part black, had enough natural identity struggles. She didn't need white people exhibiting undue anxiety over blacks. Besides, maybe the man wasn't one of the two who'd come to the front door. Maybe he was working with her husband, Marv, on the Fellowship construction crew. Maybe Marv had sent him in to use the bathroom. That was a reasonable enough possibility; it happened often with guests visiting the Fellowship for a few days.

"Okay, Penny," said Fern. "Let's go see."

The bathroom was empty, but the inside door to the basement was open. Fern was too scared to go down, so she looked out the back door of the house. The cellar door was open, and two men were leaping over the fence into the yard of the neighboring apartment building. She ducked back in and went to the dining room window overlooking the side of the house. They *were* the same men who had come in the front door.

Fern stood back from the window and watched as they casually turned into the first apartment door and stood in the entryway where she could still see them.

In a few minutes they came out of the door, and slowly strolled down the walk toward the street. Fern told the kids to stay in the house and ran out of the front door. She confronted the men just as they reached the sidewalk and turned the other way to join four other men who had apparently been waiting for them.

"Hey, what were you doing in our house?" asked Fern as she caught up to them.

"What do you mean? We weren't in your house. You're crazy, woman!"

"Hey, come on. Let's get out of here," said one of the other four.

Just then Penny came up behind Fern. "That's the one. That one was in our bathroom. That one right there." She pointed out the shorter of the two men who had come to the front door. He was about five feet, ten inches tall.

"Come on," he said nervously, turning away, and they all left.

Fern and Penny returned to the house, and in a few moments another Fellowship mother came over. When Fern had unloaded her frightening story, they both went down to the basement thinking that the men had been after the bicycles parked there. The bicycles were undisturbed, but scattered on the floor were the contents of her purse. It lay by the back steps going up to the cellar door. Missing was her checkbook and wallet with her driver's license, gas credit cards, a J. C. Penneys' credit card, $80 cash, and the house key.

They called Marv, but he was on a job and the message didn't get delivered right away. Penny and Fern were quite shaken as the intensity and shock of the situation dawned more fully on them. Penny talked a lot, paced back and forth, and frequently looked out the window to see if the men were coming back. Fern tried to keep calm for the sake of the children, but she also began to wonder if the fact that she had hassled them would cause them to come back to get revenge, to make her and Penny keep silent, or something. The scare of having been invaded in the middle of the day, right in her own home, was the worst. It was so audacious to her that it disrupted all sense of order and safety. Somehow a night burglar, an assault on a lonely street, getting ripped off on the "el" train, something of that sort, would have been more rational—to find danger where you expected it.

But to have your house invaded during the daylight, while you are there—to feel that you are completely impotent, not because the intruders are holding you at gunpoint, but because they disregard you when you try to confront them—that was totally unnerving. Where is safety?

When Marv arrived, he consulted with a few other folks and then dialed 911 to report the incident. They were not yet sure whether they would try to press charges. When the policeman came he took down their story, but said that unless they were clear that they'd press charges, there was nothing he could do. He'd wait a day or so and then tear up the report if they did not want to press charges. The police weren't going to waste their time looking for someone if they didn't have a chance of prosecution.

Before evening Marv changed the locks on their doors, and that night they locked them—something they hadn't been used to doing except when they were going to be away for a day or more.

The question about pressing charges was complicated by the fact that it appeared as though Penny would have to testify in court if the case ever came to trial. She was the only person who had actually seen the man in the bathroom, making her testimony important to the prosecution. This seemed like a hard place in which to put a child. She'd be asked to testify against a man who either lived nearby or frequented the neighborhood and could easily intimidate her. She'd had an earlier traumatic experience in court when her father was on trial and had been sent to jail briefly. She remembered how horrible that had been for him. She declared firmly that she did not want to send anybody to jail, especially somebody who had not physically hurt anyone.

The Evanston Police Department has a fine victim advocate program which assigns someone to try to understand the needs of the victims. Friday, the day following the incident, Marv and Fern contacted their victim advocate who said he would do his best to work with the state's attorney so that Penny would not have to appear in court if they pressed charges. Then, after some conversations with other elders in the Fellowship, Marv phoned the officer to whom he had initially reported the crime and told him that they were prepared to press charges. He said that he would see what he could do.

Later that day, and also on Saturday, Penny said she saw the man again who had been in their bathroom. Fern also thought she saw him. As she stopped her car at a corner, he came walking past her. He seemed to look right at her but gave no indication that he recognized her. She felt like talking to him, but didn't. What if he were the wrong man? She drove on home.

When Marv heard that both Penny and Fern thought they had seen the man who'd been in their house, he was on the lookout for anyone who fit the description. On Sunday as the family were loading items into the car to go on a picnic, Marv noticed several guys sitting in the park across the street from their house. He asked Penny to take a look and see if any of them was the one.

"Yeah, that's the one right there on the end," she said.

"Are you sure?" asked Marv.

"Of course I'm sure. I saw him in our bathroom."

Marv called Fern over to the car and asked her if any of the men looked familiar. She identified the same person with equal certainty, so they went into the house and called one of the other elders in order to have someone else involved in their consideration. Together they decided that they would call the police.

Just a few minutes after they did so a police car stopped at their house and had them identify the man in question. The officer radioed for a second car that came through the alley to the back side of the park, and the police made the arrest.

It was hard for Marv and Fern and their family to watch the police confront the man, have him put his hands up, frisk him, and then put handcuffs on him and know that the responsibility for identifying him was totally on them. It was obvious to the other people in the park that Marv and Fern had been the ones to call the police, and it was still hard to imagine what might happen if the guy was sent to prison. They hoped he was under 18. He looked like he might be. That would protect him from some of the worst prison conditions and give him the benefit and help of the good juvenile officers in Evanston.

The second man who had initially come to the front door was not in the park. Apparently he was not from the neighborhood. He was older, and didn't show up again. One of the things that had been happening in the neighborhood was that a group of older guys would come around and put pressure on the younger ones to steal for them. Marv and Fern had overheard conversations where they were yelling things like, "When I send you out after something, I want you to get me a good one. Don't you ever bring me this crap again! I can't use it, and it's not worth the risk."

Marv and Fern had to take Penny down to the police station. As the police questioned the young man, whose name was Victor, Marv and Fern prayed that Penny wouldn't be required to have to identify him formally. At first Victor denied everything. Then the police reported that he said he was never in the house but he knew who did it and could get the stuff back. From that point on he kept changing his story, and though he never admitted that he was in the house, the police were confident that they had the right person. They booked him and did not require Penny to become formally involved.

A hearing was set for the next day, but Victor asked to be represented by an attorney, so it was postponed for two weeks, and he was released on bail.

A week later Marv and Fern were walking down the sidewalk when they met Victor coming toward them by himself. Marv decided that he would try to talk with him to establish some contact.

"Hey, Victor," Marv started.

"That ain't my name," he snapped back, but he did stop. (Marv and Fern later learned that he went by Vic.)

Marv didn't know what to say or how to start, so he jumped in with, "I wonder if you're aware how it makes people feel when you come into their house uninvited?"

"Well, what do you think it feels like to be accused of something you didn't do and be picked up by the police?" he responded.

"I know what you did," said Marv. "There's no doubt in our minds, so we don't want to get into an argument about whether you were in the house. But I want you to know how that affects people, and what kind of fear that stirs up in my wife and the children. That really frightened them."

"I know what it's like. Guys break into my house all the time," he said without hostility. "But I never was in your house."

Fern said, "You know and I know that you were in our house, and Penny saw you too. There's no doubt. It's just a question of when you'll admit it."

He shook his head and laughed nervously. "I didn't have nothin' to do with it. I know, 'cause I know who was in there, and it wasn't me. Besides, how come you're so uptight this time? You didn't do anything last time someone broke into your house."

Marv and Fern were speechless. Vic was apparently referring to a burglary that had happened to them nearly a year before when they had lost a camera, tape recorder, and several other items.

Finally Marv said, "Well, we don't want to see you go to jail, but somehow we want to make sure that you don't do that again."

Vic laughed his nervous laugh, and they all turned and walked their separate ways. It didn't seem like a very well-resolved conclusion to their conversation, but later as they thought about it, Marv and Fern realized that a certain weight had lifted from them. They were basically no longer afraid. The personal contact, unresolved though it had been, had removed the fear. They talked about that and even felt that beyond the relief from the psychological fear, they were quite certain that Vic would never enter their house uninvited again.

But should they drop the charges now that their personal fears were relieved? It was a hard decision. At the police station they discovered that Vic had been convicted for a previous unlawful entry. The evidence in this case was substantial, also tending toward a conviction. He was over 18. A prison sentence was almost certain if they continued to press charges. They didn't like to think about that, but Vic himself had commented on the important social role that the criminal justice system is supposed to play in our society. It is supposed to keep order and prevent crime. In spite of the statistics which say that the threat of incarceration has little impact on the incidence of crime, here was a case in which our failure to prosecute the year before had given Vic an excuse (at least after the fact) for continuing in crime. Had our lenience done him a disservice? Had we done the neighborhood a disservice by teaching at least one young person (and probably more) that he could get away with crime?

The questions weren't easy.

Finally, as Marv and Fern discussed the question with others of us in the community, we decided to drop the charges. Our Cook County Jail and State prisons are notorious. We could not play a part in putting somebody in one of them for having taken $80 from us. We also reasoned that the little contact we had had with Vic might have been redemptive. Hopefully, we could continue to see him around the neighborhood in the future. Maybe it would make some difference. Also, even though the *threat* of prison might have deterred Vic at an earlier point, the actual *experience* of prison, of our prisons, would almost certainly instruct and involve him in more serious crime.

The state's attorney thought Marv and Fern were crazy to drop charges and said that he considered it dangerous and unwise to have initiated any kind of conversation with a defendant. The judge responded similarly when Marv and Fern announced in court that they wanted to drop charges: "So you think it is okay for someone to break into your house and take things from you if he's a neighbor, huh? What's going to stop him from doing it again? What's going to stop somebody else from doing it when they hear about what you're doing?"

Vic, who was right beside Marv and Fern as they all stood before the judge's bench, looked shocked when Marv and Fern announced their intentions not to press charges. He looked down at the floor without making any comment as the judge challenged Marv and Fern on their decision.

"Is this still what you want to do?" the judge asked.

Marv and Fern nodded.

"Very well. Case dismissed," the judge said as he whacked his gavel on the bench.

Vic, Marv, and Fern turned and walked out of court. Marv opened the door and held it for Fern and Vic.

"Hey, thanks a lot," said Vic in a quiet voice.

Fern couldn't respond because of feeling overwhelmed by the whole situation. They stood on the courthouse steps. Vic said that it was true that he had been the one who had come into their house. And even though he wouldn't say who his partner had been, he did admit that he was in the bathroom, had taken the money, jumped over the fence—the whole thing.

"It's not so much the point that you took off with my purse," Fern said, "even though that's wrong, but the main thing that really affected me was the fear of being invaded."

"Yeah, I can understand that," answered Vic.

"I wish I knew that that would never happen again," said Fern.

"Well, I can give you my word on that," said Vic.

They talked further. Marv asked him if he needed a job. He did, but still had some ideas he was planning to pursue. Before they parted, Vic said that he had turned Fern's wallet and everything except the money in to the police, covering himself with the story that he'd gotten it from a friend. He thought they could get it from the police now that the case was over.

Throughout the rest of the summer Marv and Fern saw Vic often in the park or on the street. He was always friendly and open. From time to time he tried to do nice things for the kids when they were present, like buying them ice cream or pushing them in the swings. Maybe it had struck him how much he had scared them. Penny was always nervous around him, but she would speak to him.

Vic finally got a job and didn't spend his days hanging around the streets any longer. A year later, after not seeing him for some time, Fern met him one day.

"How are you doing?" she asked.

"Much better, much better. I moved, ya' know, but I'm still workin'. How about you?"

"Fine. I'm doin' fine."

3
Sexual Deviants

This morning the nude body of a woman was found lying in the backyard of some neighbors who live just around the corner. Apparently, the attractive 22-year-old woman had been abducted from in front of her apartment about six blocks away around 2:45 a.m. The police think she was held captive through the remainder of the night, raped, and then murdered shortly before 7:00 a.m. when her body was found by someone out walking his dog.

The trail of blood across the sidewalk and grass suggests that the killer unloaded the woman's body from a car and dragged it to the yard. The police found her clothing piled in the alley about 100 feet away along with her purse, still containing about $25. Because there was no blood on her clothes, they think the two stab wounds in her chest happened after she had been disrobed.

We are all in shock!

∘ ∘ ∘

I wrote down the details about that crime the evening of the day that it was discovered. Several months have now elapsed, but it remains unsolved. Three days after the

woman's body was found, the 63-year-old night-manager of
our local newsstand was shot and killed in an apparent robbery attempt shortly after closing at midnight. Before three
weeks were out a total of three murders and six rapes had
rocked our small city—the largest rash of violent crime in its
history.

But a bizarre series of such violent crimes was not un-
precedented. During the summer of '77, there was a sequence of rapes adding up to 12 by mid-August. Several
took place in our immediate neighborhood, one in the building across the street.

Police detectives went from door to door asking if anyone
had seen the red VW that the assailant of the woman across
the street had reportedly driven. He fit the description of the
rapist in three other cases.

Finally, the police did locate and arrest a suspect, charg-
ing him with four of the rapes in our area. The victims were
able to identify him. He turned out to be a paroled rapist
who had been released from prison only a few months
earlier.

As time went on the police made other arrests, but that
year the safety that we usually presume in our neighborhood
was uncertain.

Sometimes we've had the impression that God holds the
forces of evil at bay, even in a geographical way, in our
neighborhood. However, the statistics don't show that to be
so. Maybe in terms of spiritual warfare this is more of a battlefield than a fortification, and yet we usually *feel* safe.
Whether it is God's supernatural protection of us or the fact
that on the street we usually pass people who love us and familiar homes with open shades, warm lights, and welcoming
faces, makes little difference. It is all a gift from God.

But that year evil was on a hit-and-run spree in our neighborhood and everyone felt jumpy. Earlier in the year three children were abducted from our part of town. One of the girls was a young child from the Fellowship.

It happened on her way home from school for lunch one noon. A man claiming to be a newspaper photographer doing a story on families took several pictures of her and two friends. Then, explaining that he was going to take her home to get some pictures of the family, he steered her into his car and drove off. He pulled a knife from the back seat and threatened her with it if she didn't crouch down under the dashboard as he drove along. He stopped in an alley near the lake and made her sit near him for a while. Then he released her unharmed at a nearby beach approximately one half hour after picking her up. She wandered about, lost and afraid, until a woman walking her dog found her and called her parents.

Though the police worked hard and even brought in one suspect whom they thought fit the description, no arrests were made because none of the three girls could positively identify the man as the molester.

In situations like this where innocent and defenseless victims are threatened, who would hesitate even a moment to invite the aid and protection of the police? In fact, as ugly as prison is, almost no one would prefer that such a disturbed person be free to move about without some guarantee that no other innocent person will suffer.

The feelings that rise within us are too strong to be restrained. Oh yes, there are lots of social and psychological reasons why a person becomes a criminal. And when the victim is a distant statistic, we may have some sympathy for the criminal and blame society or even ourselves. But when you know the victim, your feelings can justify a harsh response to the criminal. If he is sane, you hold him accountable no matter what his background might have been. If he is emotionally deranged, you still want him confined.

Are those feelings base, the product of our fallen nature, a thinly disguised thirst for vengeance? Or are they normal, God-given responses designed to motivate us to create governments which can protect us from such abuses, even by force? Of course if there were no sin, such protection would not be necessary. But there is sin, and there is that kind of crime, so how should the Christian behave?

Encounters with exhibitionists have also involved us with sexual deviants. In one situation a couple of Fellowship women were down near the lake having a picnic in the park one summer afternoon. As they sat on either side of a picnic table a man walked up behind one of the women, exposed himself, and began to masturbate.

The woman facing the man from the other side of the table told her friend not to turn around, then she boldly said to the man, "In the name of Jesus Christ, leave!"

We have heard of many stories in which people who were in dangerous situations were able to call upon the authority of the Lord to renounce the evil. Sometimes it has stopped assailants cold or frightened them away. This time the man replied, "In the name of Jesus Christ, come," as he completed his act. Then he departed.

The women were physically unharmed but very shaken. It was some time before their sense of peace returned.

There have been other incidents with exhibitionists. One involved my wife, Neta. One day when she turned into the parking lot of a nearby store, she looked up to see an exhibitionist standing in a back doorway immediately in front of her car. She left and reported the incident to the police.

The detective who came to our house to make a report

said he was quite certain who the offender was from the location and previous offenses, but Neta was not able to identify his picture from the mug book.

The officer said that in any case he would pay a visit to the man to talk to him. He wanted to encourage him to get into therapy. We appreciated this approach which not only showed concern for the protection of society but considered the welfare of the offender.

4
Reflections I: Distinctions

Maybe the most valuable aspect of reviewing our actual experiences with crime and violence is that they help us face reality. But the greatest liability in doing so may be our tendency to justify *whatever* we have done in those times of crisis and emotion. So we must also challenge our experiences by the ideals we believe God has shown us.

God's ideals and reality do not contradict each other. Therefore we must bring them together and wrestle with the paradox. To begin with, if we must call the police, we should do so without evading our share of the responsibility for what might happen—to the offender in prison for years to come or to society if he is later released as a trained and angry criminal. On the other hand, if we don't call the police, we must reject any illusions about the miracles we can work or the price we and our neighbors might have to pay for that decision.

In searching for realism at Reba Place we have noted a number of helpful distinctions. They are not principles upon which we feel we must act, but they help give us a clearer idea of the choices we face. Where God gives us the faith to act beyond what seems indicated by the natural facts, we can do that with less sentimentality and grandiosity. Some of the distinctions are as follows:

1. *Juvenile versus **adult** crime*. In our city we have some fine juvenile officers. We've learned to know some of them personally, and we've seen them talk with wisdom to young people who have gotten in trouble. Several steps are taken toward correcting the young person before he faces a judge. Even when juveniles are arrested, the courts often exercise other options before sending them to reformatory. Calling the police when a young person has broken the law can be an important step in the youth's training and education. Sometimes the young person doesn't know that what he is doing is really *that* wrong or that anything serious will happen. Not calling the police can in some cases shield him from reality.

Hardened or street-wise youths are, however, more like adults. The courts may still treat them with leniency, but such persons can take advantage of that by calculating what they can get away with. They are not receptive to the discipline of facing up to society's expectations. They've already had that education without a positive effect.

The main difference between a juvenile and an adult is that if the adult is convicted and has a previous record, he is likely to have to serve time. In spite of all the efforts to make our penal system a place for rehabilitation and reform, it continues to fail. Maybe such a paternalistic role toward adults can never succeed. If an adult *decides* to quit crime, some form of rehabilitation may facilitate the individual's efforts at making a new life. But an adult must make such a decision on his own.

This distinction between juveniles and adults recognizes some differences in the way they may be treated. Other differences may sometimes occur in a negative way for racial minorities. In some situations racial minorities may not be treated fairly. One may choose not to call the police if he thinks the offender might be mistreated or not receive justice because of discrimination. A decision not to call the police should not be made on the basis of all the hardships minority people have experienced. If the person has committed a crime, he is a criminal, and sentimentality about how his background justifies his actions is an encouragement to more crime. But realism about whether the person will be treated justly may help one decide whether or not to press charges.

2. *Crimes against persons versus crimes against property.* To have your home burglarized while you are away can feel like a terrible violation, but it is nothing to the terror of being robbed while you are home. And, of course, assault or rape is even more serious. The law recognizes these distinctions in terms of the severity of sentences. Also the police sometimes recognize the differences in terms of how diligently they investigate the various crimes. As a victim it is useful to remind oneself of these differences.

If you've lost something that you prize highly or cannot replace, it may not occur to you to be grateful that you and others are physically safe. But any decision based on this distinction should not deny the seriousness of what has happened. Crimes against property are serious too. And any time we decide not to prosecute or call the police, we should make sure we are not just wanting to avoid thinking about the pain and shock of what has happened. One good test is to consider whether we are willing to engage the offender in some more redemptive way. Would we stop him on the street and talk to him about what has happened, seeking some resolution?

3. *The rational criminal versus the insane person.* One

who chooses to break the law is quite different from the person who cannot help himself. Without answering the question of how one should respond to the rational and determined criminal, the person who is insane, drunk, or a drug addict needs help for his or her own sake. Contrary to the public image of how the law deals with those kinds of people—considering their problem as an excuse for their criminal behavior—we believe that there is more Christian justification for stepping in and doing something for these people. On the other hand, the more choice a person exercises in executing a crime, the more he falls into the category of the "enemy," and the more Jesus' teachings on nonresistance apply.

Some behavioral scientists try to make the case that everyone's actions are predetermined and that free choice plays little part in the decisions any of us make, dismissing culpability for even the "rational" criminal. So where is the difference? A simple difference can be found in asking yourself, will such persons thank me for intervening when they are in their right mind?

We have restrained, subdued, called the police, and helped hospitalize people who have later thanked us for preventing them from doing further damage to themselves or others.

Theoretically, if a "rational" criminal were truly rehabilitated by prison to live a happy and law-abiding life, he might thank whoever had him arrested. And that sometimes happens, but it is rare enough to note a distinction between the two types of people.

4. *Crimes against others versus crimes against ourselves.* We may turn our other cheek to the person who violates us, but it is another matter to turn our neighbor's cheek. In our Christian community we have made certain commitments

to a simple lifestyle in order to break the hold that possessions can have on people. We'd prefer to lay up treasure in heaven "where thieves do not break in and steal." But that is a voluntary choice, and even though thieves may trouble those who place more trust in earthly goods, we cannot overlook that crime. Sometimes when Christian radicals preach against materialism, they sound as though they've forgotten that theft, robbery, and vandalism are sins just like greed and selfishness. The glorification of a "Robin Hood" is not a biblical theme.

Part of our kingdom ethic is the belief that God will meet our needs, often through other Christians. In our community that happens in practical ways many times when persons lose some necessity or have money stolen from them. The brothers and sisters contribute to a replacement. Other people may collect from an insurance company, but that should never cause us to feel that theft makes no difference.

We should not forget that even when we choose to turn the other cheek for ourselves, we may make crime more safe or productive for the criminal. That too can affect our neighbors.

5. *Deadly or offensive force versus restraining or diverting force.* I've known for a long time that English "bobbies" don't carry guns, but when I went through British customs for the first time and saw a pair of bobbies in the airport terminal building, I was really impressed with how different they are from the average American policeman. It wasn't just their quaint domed hats. It was their whole demeanor. They were strolling casually with their hands clasped typically (as I later learned) behind their backs, and they were smiling at people. They truly looked like *peace*-keepers and helpers.

In contrast I remembered the West Side of Chicago a few years before. At that time, if a fight or some other kind of trouble broke out in the black neighborhood, people hesitated to call the police—that is, unless they really wanted to see someone get hurt. I think things have changed somewhat now, but the likelihood of violence is a significant factor in calling the police. How committed are the police to not hurting anyone, even the person they apprehend?

On a personal level this distinction might have relevance. One day some of the elders at the Fellowship were having a conversation with John Howard Yoder, an Anabaptist theologian who has thought and written extensively on issues of peace. We were talking about crime and violence on our streets and some of the problems our children face in school, when John asked, "Have you ever thought about judo?"

"No," we answered, a little shocked. "Why?"

Judo, sometimes referred to as "the gentle art" or "conquering by yielding," was developed by the Lama monks of ancient China as a protection against robbers. The monks' ethical code prohibited weapons or intentional injury to anyone, even enemies. So they developed methods of parrying blows and throwing an opponent which was supposedly designed not to injure the assailant.

"Have you ever wondered whether some nonlethal method would be consistent with Jesus' teaching?" John asked.

In spite of judo's initial development in China, its evolution in Japan and in modern times has made it more than a nonviolent sequence of evasive maneuvers. Now it is also offensive and, except when practiced as a sport, can be deadly. John made it clear that he was not necessarily recommending that we use judo, but he was encouraging us to think about distinctions and alternatives.

The Hutterites, who have maintained a nonviolent witness for over 450 years, fled Nikolsburg, Austria, in 1528. At that time they were known as "Stäbler" (staff-bearers) in contrast to others in the town known as "Schwertler" (sword-bearers). According to *The Mennonite Encyclopedia*, one of the first historical descriptions of them appears in Caspar Franck's 1576, *Catalogus Haereticorum:* "Stäbler teach that a Christian cannot with a clear conscience and according to the Word of God bear a sword or wage war, but shall let a staff suffice."

But suffice for what? Only as an aid for walking? Or would they have felt free to use it as a quarterstaff, to ward off blows or drive off an attacker, satisfied that serious injury or death was not likely? This is not an argument in favor of various forms of "soft" defense but an observation regarding possible distinctions we might make when faced with crime and violence.

The five considerations noted above regarding various kinds of crime, different persons, varying probabilities for justice, and different personal responses do not suggest what one should do in every situation. But they help one face reality and reflect on appropriate responses for peaceful Christians.

5
Neighborhood Trust

When Ern arose at five in the morning to get ready for work he was still a little hung over from too much drinking the night before. So he took a couple drinks, hoping to soothe his throbbing head into a soft buzz. Then he discovered that he did not have a clean uniform to put on.

"Josie!" he yelled. "Where's my clothes?"°

"Huh? They're in the laundry basket. What are you doing waking me up, anyway?"

Ern found them and got out the ironing board. The delay was going to make him late. He took another drink and plugged in the iron. While it was heating, he took another drink.

"Damn woman!" Then he yelled into the bedroom. "Hey, how come you didn't iron my uniform?"

"Because I didn't have time. Now shut up, and let me go back to sleep."

"What do you mean you didn't have time? Why do you

° This first conversation between Ern and Josie is constructed around the events of the morning, though the actual words may have been different.

think I work all day—so you can sit home and do nothin'?"

"Work? Is that what you were doing last night? You sure didn't smell like it when you came home. I thought they was still puttin' gas in cars these days."

"Don't get smart with me, woman. You get out of bed and come in here and fix my uniform." And with that Ern threw the iron across the room and through the bedroom door toward where Josie lay.

She screamed and jumped out of bed. Then she grabbed their baby, the youngest of three children, and ran out of the apartment. She went upstairs to her mother's apartment and called the police.

When the police came, Ern opened the door only a crack and recognized the two black policemen who were standing there. They'd given him a hard time a few months before when he had been driving a cab. He slammed the door and told them to leave, that it was a private affair and none of their business.

"We received a call about some trouble," they said. "We just want to come in and talk to you."

"You got a warrant?"

"We're just comin' in to talk to you."

"You come through that door, and I'll shoot both of you. I know you dudes. You was the ones who muscled me around when I was drivin' cab."

"Now cool down. We're comin' in. We just want to see that everything is okay."

"Everything's cool. My wife ain't even here; so get out of here. I swear, if you try to come in, I'll shoot you."

The police called for support, then moved back, down the stairs, and outside. Sure enough, they could see through the window that Ern did have an automatic pistol. In a matter of minutes several cars of support police arrived, including the officers that were assigned to the SWAT Team (Special Weapons And Tactics). And almost as quickly as the police arrived, the media descended upon the scene with photographers, reporters, sound crews, and mini-cams. Soon in-progress reports were being broadcast every few minutes all over the Chicago area.

Walt Jones, a member of Reba Place Fellowship, was listening to the radio as he prepared to go to work. Immediately he recognized Ern's name and the address—one of the Fellowship apartment buildings in which we rent about half of the apartments to non-Fellowship people. Earlier Walt and his family had lived in the same building. In fact, his apartment and Ern's had shared the same stairwell. Walt and Ern had never learned to know each other intimately, but they were fairly well acquainted.

Walt was shocked at the radio report. Ern was such a likeable guy. Walt stepped out his back door into the courtyard where he could see the building in which Ern lived. There in the alley some of the police were staked out. Walt walked over to them and asked them what was happening. They told him and then asked, "Do you know the guy?"

"Yeah, I know him," Walt answered. "And I'm concerned about his welfare because this is a Fellowship building and he is one of our tenants."

"Would you be willing to talk to him?"

Without thinking Walt said, "Sure," and started to walk up to the building. On either side of Ern's back door stood the two policemen who had earlier attempted to enter by way of the front. They were pressed up against the wall with their guns raised in a classic break-in pose.

"Get back, get back," they warned as Walt started up the steps.

Ern was in the back part of the apartment at that point, and when Walt caught sight of him, he called out, "Ern, this is Walt from across the alley. Do you remember who I am?"

"Yeah, I remember."

"Well, I'd like to talk to you. I'm really concerned about your welfare, and maybe we can work out something with the police."

"Well," said Ern, "these guys—they got to get out of here. I know them. I know them. They're gonna get me if I come out there."

"Well, can I come in?"

"Not in this door. Come in the front where I can keep you covered."

"Sure," Walt said and backed away. His legs were starting to shake a little, but he went around to the front of the building. The police had the whole block cordoned off. Snipers were positioned on the roofs of the apartments across the street. TV cameras and more police were poking around every corner.

Walking between two buildings to get to the front, Walt was already inside the police line. They were surprised when they saw him. "Hold it," they ordered.

"It's okay," Walt said boldly and walked quickly right into the entryway of the building before the police could stop him. A sergeant in plain clothes followed him and explained that they were waiting for the chief to arrive before they did anything else. Walt explained that this was one of the Fellowship buildings and that he felt he could be of help if he went in and that Ern was willing to allow him in.

The sergeant said that if that was the case, he wanted to go in also.

"Wait a minute," Walt said, and went back outside and

called up to Ern to tell him that a policeman wanted to come in also.

"You can come in," said Ern. "But if you want to bring that cop, that's on you. If he has a gun on him or anything that looks threatening, I'll shoot you both."

Walt went back in and said to the sergeant, "He says you can go in if you are not armed. Now, I'm going to make sure you aren't armed."

The sergeant gave his gun to another officer and allowed Walt to frisk him, and they went up the stairs to the door. After they knocked on Ern's door, they had to wait ten or fifteen minutes while Ern gave them all kinds of instructions about how they were to enter, what he would allow to be discussed, and what a tough Vietnam veteran he was.

"Now I've got an M-16 right here and I can wipe out half of this block. You know that, don't you?"

"Yeah," said the sergeant.

"Well, when you come, walk in one at a time and turn immediately to your left. Don't turn to your right, and don't look behind you."

Every once in a while Ern would pull the slide back on the weapon he had so that Walt and the sergeant could hear it click. As the discussion continued Walt and the sergeant were less and less sure that they wanted to go in.

"Maybe you're too uptight for us to come in right now," said the sergeant.

"Yeah, maybe that's true," said Ern through the door. "I might get jumpy and shoot you."

But Walt wasn't ready to give up, even though he was scared. "I think the children should come out, Ern. Then we can talk about things after they are safe."

"Not a chance," yelled back Ern. "They're my protection. Once I let them go, the cops will start shootin'."

"Well, let us in to talk about their safety, at least," said Walt.

So Ern unbolted the door and allowed them to come in. He told them to stand in the center of the living room facing the couch. Ern had the sergeant place his radio on the floor. When he was satisfied that they were both unarmed, Ern allowed them to turn around and sit down.

Ern stood hunched over in the center of the room and explained that he was a black-belt in karate and could knock a fly out of the air with his toe. He gave a few demonstration kicks that convinced the sergeant that his claims had substance. The kicks also revealed that there was a pistol sticking out of his back pocket, and the belligerence that had been in the sergeant's voice melted.

With the sergeant humbled, Walt felt more secure and took the initiative to talk about his own concern as a neighbor and Christian. "I'm sure the Lord loves you," Walt said. "I know He's concerned about all of your difficulties and wants to protect you and your family. And I sure wouldn't want to see you harmed."

Ern accepted that and began to talk about his concerns. While he talked the stress he was under became more and more evident. His mood would change from compassion to anger to fear to cooperation. A couple of times he started crying and became completely irrational. Finally, he focused on the fact that he wanted the two policemen who had come to his door initially to leave the scene entirely. If they didn't leave, he would refuse to talk.

With the approval of the sergeant and Ern, Walt reached for the radio and communicated the message to the policemen outside. In a few moments the officers that Ern had objected to came around to the front where he could see them, got into a squad car, and drove off.

Then the sergeant, who was white, got into an argument with Ern about who was the toughest and who had experienced the most hand-to-hand combat in Vietnam. Ern got all stirred up again and went into several demonstrations of his abilities. This time instead of subduing the sergeant, the spectacle of a black man exercising such power and authority over him infuriated the sergeant and he argued more intensely. Soon it became a racial argument.

Walt, who had grown up as a member of a black gang in the Harlem ghetto, knew that the situation was getting dangerous. But this was not a time to call upon his old skills as a street fighter or his own experience in the military. Those were his old ways. In his new life, he was serious about his commitment to nonviolence and his desire to bring the Lord and His peace into a situation.

The children had come into the room and had gravitated over to Walt. One was sitting on his lap. Finally, in an attempt to distract the other two men from their argument, Walt stood up slowly and said that he thought it was time to get the children out of the situation because they were hungry and tired and scared.

"You don't tell me what to do with my children," Ern shouted. "You kids get back in the bedroom and shut the door."

Walt sat back down and started to pray out loud. He confessed that he didn't know what to do but affirmed his certainty of the Lord's presence and love for Ern and concern for his welfare. While Walt was praying the sergeant made a couple of attempts to say something, but Ern refused to answer him. Walt looked up to see Ern standing there with his hand held out toward the sergeant to silence him during the prayer. Then Walt finished praying.

"Do you consider yourself a Christian?" Walt asked Ern.

"Yes, I'm a Christian. I've been a Christian all my life."

"Well, I feel that the Lord really cares for you and is not going to allow you to be harmed, so I'm going to get up now, and I'm going to go get the children and take them outside. I'd be willing to come back and walk with you so that you could come out too."

"No! They'd shoot me."

"I'll tell you what," Walt said. "I'll get a senior elder from our church to come back with me."

"Could you do that?"

"Right away," Walt said and picked up the police radio to request that one of the senior elders be found. Then Walt went for the children and walked them to the door. Ern made no effort to stop him. The door was locked. Walt was nervous and had to struggle with the sticky bolt to get it open. All the time the kids kept asking where they were going.

"Just come on," was all Walt could say as he hurried out the door and down the stairs, with each step imagining a bullet splatting into the back of his head.

Outside the door, the scene was unreal. A cluster of police stood in the middle of the street. Behind them on the other side and in a semicircle to both sides was a wall of people. Rising above the crowd were the little towers of the television mini-cam trucks with microwave dish antennas on top. On top of the buildings were the SWAT snipers.

Walt took the children to Josie who was standing off to the side; she had never expected things to escalate so far and fast. Walt began to realize what a victory the Lord had given just to get the children out without harm to anyone. Then he looked off to his left and saw Julius Belser, one of the senior elders of the Fellowship. Walt went over to him and explained the situation, saying that he believed that Ern would come out if he and Julius would escort him.

Walt and Julius went in the building together and up to Ern's apartment. Ern and the sergeant were out in the hall when they arrived.

"Ern, this is Julius Belser. He's one of our senior elders, and he loves the Lord. He's here for your protection."

Ern grabbed Julius' extended hand firmly with both of his hands and said in a loud and intense voice, "Do you know the Lord?"

"Yes," Julius said with a big smile and then put Ern's hand under his arm and turned and started down the steps. Walt followed, and the sergeant came last. Ern had left his gun in the apartment.

Once outside the door, Julius, Ern, and Walt walked directly to the street where a police car was waiting at the curb. No one handcuffed Ern or anything. They all got in, and the police drove them to the station, recognizing the role that Walt and Julius were playing in assuring Ern of his safety.

While they were riding along Walt said, "Ern, you've really shown yourself to be a loving father by putting your children's safety before your own. I think that's the kind of person God wants us to be because He's a loving Father. I think He's demonstrating His love for you by not allowing you to be harmed and by giving us to you for your protection as a result of your faith in Him."

It was reassuring to Ern to hear that Walt accepted the authenticity of his faith in Jesus. It was good to be reminded of God's continued presence. Walt and Julius prayed with him and promised that one of them would stay with him as long as possible.

When they got to the station, the police ushered them into an office. Seated around a desk, they began to discuss with a detective and the state's attorney what was to happen. The detective was an understanding black man with sensitivity to the amount of humiliation and confusion that Ern was experiencing. He kept the press out so they wouldn't harass Ern.

Finally, instead of all the serious charges that might have been brought against Ern, the authorities decided to charge him with only three misdemeanors: assault, disorderly conduct, and possession of an unregistered weapon. Because the charges were relatively minor, they decided to ask the judge for only $1,000 bail. Those decisions were small miracles. Ern had most of the $100 (the required 10%) for bail with him. Julius and Walt arranged to pay the remainder.

Then another miracle happened. The case load in the Evanston court was too heavy for Ern to be arraigned within any reasonable time. So, instead of putting Ern in jail until a judge could see him, they arranged for him to be arraigned in neighboring Skokie. And his case was sandwiched right into the day's schedule so that there was no unnecessary waiting.

The police did handcuff Ern to take him into another court situation, but he accepted that without a struggle. He was beginning to realize how much grace he'd been given. He wasn't dead. His family was safe. He hadn't been shot at. No one had punched him or even yelled at him. He had been treated with respect and charged with crimes far less serious than those he'd committed.

When Ern was called before the judge, the state's attorney explained the situation and stated that he was bringing three charges and asking for $1,000 bail. He told the judge that a representative from a church in Ern's neighborhood would like to say a few words. (Since it had not seemed necessary for two people to be present, Julius had not gone along to the court in Skokie.) Walt stepped forward and explained that he was from Reba Place and that we owned the building in which Ern and his family lived and that we'd be willing to do anything we could to help Ern out at this hard time.

"Would your church be willing to offer this couple some marriage counseling?" the judge asked.

"We certainly would."

"Okay. Put up the bail, begin the counseling, and see the clerk to set a trial date." Bang! The gavel came down, and the judge called for the next case.

The detectives drove Walt and Ern, not only back to Evanston, but right to the corner of Ern's apartment. They talked freely all the way. When they arrived, Ern was able to get out, be seen by his neighbors, and return home without any harm that same afternoon. Considering the way Ern had started the morning, it was truly a miracle.

A few weeks later on the day scheduled for the trial, Walt went with Ern and Josie. The public defender thought that the best plan would be for Ern to plead guilty and ask for a suspended sentence. But when they checked that out with the state's attorney (a different one this time), she just laughed and said that Ern was going to jail. At that point Walt explained that our church was really interested in him and that we'd been counseling with the family. He said that we'd really feel good about taking on some responsibility.

"Oh, oh," she said. "Well, that's a little different." Then after thinking about it a little while, she said, "There's one thing we might be able to do. It's not common, but it is called a 'deferred sentence.' At the end of a year, Ern would have to return to court and, contingent upon a good report, he could be released. During that year he would remain under the supervision of the court, be examined by a court psychiatrist periodically, and be instructed to receive marriage counseling from Reba Place Fellowship.''

When they went before the judge, the state's attorney proposed that creative plan, and the judge agreed.

During the first few weeks things were touch and go. Two or three times Ern and Josie got into big arguments that threatened to erupt into another physical fight. The counseling team was called in and tried to work things out. Occasionally they told Ern to spend the night at someone else's house until he and Josie could cool down. That was hard for him to agree to do.

But in time, through the regular counseling sessions, Ern and Josie discovered many of the sources of their conflicts. They had believed that they were fundamentally incompatible, but the counseling revealed that their problems were more their habit of taking advantage of each other emotionally. That insight led to some foundational changes, and they have learned to communicate much better. Ern has stopped his excessive drinking and comes directly home from work at night. He's reduced his long hours and doesn't spend a lot of time hanging out with his buddies since he no longer feels the need to stay out of the house.

Ern and Josie decided that they didn't just want *professional* counseling to help them manage their conflicts and get along better. They've asked for *Christian* counseling to learn how to bring the Lord into the decisions of their lives.

Ern manages a gas station. Recently, when he was the only person on duty for his turn on the night shift, a gunman robbed the station. Ern could hardly resist trying to overpower the gunman because of his pride in being the toughest guy around and highly skilled in karate. "The only thing that kept me from making a move on that dude was the fact that I was able to think of my wife and children," he said later. "I've never been able to do that before. I've always had to meet the challenge no matter what the risk. This time I thought of how they would be hurt if something went wrong and I ended up in the hospital."

6
Give to Him Who Asks

Joan Vogt is the household manager of L'Hayim, one of our extended family households. Her husband, Virgil Vogt, is one of the elders of the Fellowship. On a Wednesday evening the members of the household and other adults making up the L'Hayim Small Group were preparing for their midweek meeting when Joan noticed through the window a light in the garage behind their house.

They had done a lot of work in one half of their garage to create a play gym for kids. A heater keeps it warm on chilly days; old rugs soften the floor. Perched in the rafters is a clubhouse with a ladder to reach it and a rope to swing down. Fresh paint brightens the walls, and an old record player sits in the corner for the kids to use.

Joan slipped out the back door to go turn off the light, thinking that one of the kids had left it on.

When she entered the gym, she met two men. One was holding the record player, while the other one was trying to get one of the small detachable speakers down from the nail on the wall where it hung.

The man holding the stereo said, "He came to get his stereo," referring to the man trying to get the speaker down.

"What do you mean? That's our stereo," said Joan.

"No, this guy said it was his, and we just came to pick it up."

"Oh no. This stereo belongs to us," she answered. "But if you think you need this stereo more than we do, let's go into the house and talk about it. Actually, it's not very good. That's why we had it out here for the kids to use. But if you really want it, let's talk."

The men were so dumbfounded that they just looked at Joan, mumbling that it belonged to one of them.

"Come on, let's go into the house," Joan insisted as she took one of the men by the arm and began to move toward the door. Even though Joan is just a medium-sized woman, the man panicked at that point, probably presuming that she would call the police once she had him inside the house. He hit Joan on the jaw and nearly knocked her down. They dropped the stereo and ran.

After they were gone, the fright of the situation began to set in. "But somehow during the whole experience I wasn't afraid," Joan said. "I never would have gone out there if I had known anybody was in the garage. I'm not a brave sort of person. In fact, ever since that event, I don't like to go out there alone in the dark.

"Just last night I looked out and noticed that the light was on. Instead of going out myself, I asked one of the men in the household if he'd turn out the light. But on the night of the stereo incident, I didn't feel any fear. I was startled when I met those men, yet somehow I knew that the Lord was with me. I was really shocked at myself later when I realized what I had done."

It has been a lot more frightening to Joan on other occasions when thieves have come right into their house. Two times Joan and Virgil were awakened by the barking of their little dog, Harpo. Once Joan went down the front stairs to find a man standing in the entryway about to grab her purse hanging from the back of a chair. Upon seeing her, he ran out of the house without taking anything.

On the other occasion, she and Virgil went down the back stairs to find the back door and yard gate propped open and Harpo chasing two men down the alley with his furious yapping. The men had apparently intended to steal the ten-speed bicycles locked in the basement. (An organized bike-theft ring was operating in our neighborhood at the time.)

Later, thieves did succeed in taking some expensive, borrowed recording equipment and a calculator from the basement.

In recalling the stereo incident, Joan is not sure why she offered to talk about giving the stereo to the potential thief. She thinks the idea may have come from remembering an incident that happened sometime before with Gary Havens, another Fellowship member.

∘ ∘ ∘

Gary and his family were living as a nuclear family in one of the two double flats owned by the Fellowship. He was employed as a landscaper, which meant that he left for work early in the morning. But when the project for the day was completed, he often arrived home in the early afternoon.

About three o'clock on a warm afternoon Gary walked into his first floor apartment to find no one home. His wife, Jan, had taken the kids to the nearby park to play. Gary noticed that the speakers of their stereo component system were turned around.

Just then Jan and the kids came in the front door. After greeting them, Gary said, "What's with the stereo speakers?"

"Well, that's something I want to talk to you about. I think that somebody was in our house this afternoon. A little while ago I came in to get some things and found the back door open. Somebody had gone into our bedroom and rummaged through the little oriental keepsake chest on our dresser."

"Well, did they take anything?"

"I don't think they took anything out of there, but they took all the money out of our penny jar. They took that big old bread knife, and they even took some popsicles that I had made for the kids right out of the freezing compartment. And I noticed the stereo speakers turned around."

"What did you do?"

"I was just on my way to get someone when I saw you come home, so I followed you back here."

"Well, I'm going to repair that front door lock so that you can close this place up when you're gone," said Gary.

While Jan took the kids back to the park, Gary found some tools and began to take the front door apart. There was still plenty of afternoon left, and he figured that he could go to the hardware store for a new tumbler or whatever was needed.

Not knowing that Gary had returned home, the people who had entered the house apparently saw Jan and the kids return to the park and presumed that the house was again empty. While Gary was kneeling behind the furniture, quietly working on the front door lock, he heard someone on the back porch. He peered around the corner until he could see three black teenage boys looking in the window.

Without thinking about a plan of action, Gary bolted through the house for the back door. The intruders jumped off the porch and started running through the yard for the alley. Gary, dressed in the tennis shoes and shorts he had worn to work that day because it was so warm, sped after them.

When they got to the corner, the boys were smart enough to break up and go in three directions. Gary stayed on the trail of one of them. The kid ran through yards and over fences, and for a while Gary wasn't sure he could keep pace. But he decided that wherever the kid could go, he could go, so Gary kept running. In about a block and a half, Gary began to notice that he was gaining on the kid. The boy's pants didn't have a belt and were slipping down just enough to inhibit his running.

When Gary caught up with him, he tackled the kid, and they both went tumbling down the alley. Several black neighbors out on the porches of their apartments observed what had happened and started yelling, wanting to know what was happening.

"You leave that kid alone, or we'll call the police," one called out.

"That's okay. You do that," Gary yelled back. "This kid was burgling my house."

"No I wasn't," yelled the boy. "Some other kids were on his back porch, and we went up there just to see what they were doing. I didn't do nothin'."

"Just leave those white people alone," yelled the neighbor. "Stay away from those white people."

Gary stood the kid up and said, "Come on, we're going back to my house. I want to talk to you." Sheepishly, the kid dropped his hostility and went along with Gary.

Somewhere in the run or fall, the boy had scratched his arm, so when they got to the house, Gary gave him an opportunity to clean up the scratch. Then they sat and talked. Gary introduced himself, and the boy also told his name. Gary tried to portray what it felt like to have one's home broken into and the fear and insecurity this could engender in his children to realize that they weren't safe. And then Gary asked what the boys had done with the things that they had taken.

Apparently the kid was afraid that Gary was going to call the police, so he cooperated by telling where they had stashed the old knife and admitting that they had eaten the popsicles. Gary interrupted the kid to assure him that he did not intend to call the police. In spite of his relief, the boy continued to tell how they had spent the pennies on hamburgers and hotdogs. The more they talked, the more Gary came to feel that this kid was not the instigator, but had probably just gone along with the others. Gary was about to tell the kid that he could leave, when he remembered the stereo and thought he should say more.

"You know, all of these things are property of the church and therefore belong to God. I'm not necessarily wanting to protect them and keep them for myself. If you want some of these things, you're not free to take them, but you can ask for them. Then we can talk to some of the elders about who needs them more. Maybe God does want you to have something that's now here in my house, but you're not free just to walk in and take it."

Gary admonished the kid never to break into somebody's house again, and then they said good-bye.

The next day, however, Gary felt the weight of the whole ordeal descend upon him in a new way. Their home had been violated. It was hard to accept, hard not to be angry and want to retaliate. It seemed like he had done what a Christian should do the day before, but he didn't feel good about it. He wasn't released from the event. Even though he'd had contact with the boy, he still felt anxious about the safety of his family. He prayed several times during the day that the Lord would do something to bring the event to closure or to bring something good out of it.

That evening when Gary arrived home from work, Jan announced that during the day she had been visited by the Evanston Police. Gary couldn't figure out how that could have happened since he had not reported the incident. Jan said that a nice-looking black detective had come to the door. After identifying himself, he had asked to come in and talk.

As the story unfolded, the boy Gary had talked to the day before felt so bad about what he had done that when he got home he talked to his mother about the incident. She was so irate that she took him to the police and made him tell them about the whole incident.

The police were aware of the identity of the other kids involved in the burglary. The gang had been involved with a number of other incidents. But this experience gave the police the opportunity to go to the boys' parents and help them to get the kids back under control. The policeman was grateful for the chance to intervene, and he had just dropped by to inform Jan and Gary of the outcome.

A couple nights later when Jan and Gary returned home from a Fellowship meeting, their babysitter said that a kid had come to the door and said that he was interested in looking at the stereo that was being given away. The babysitter said, "Well, you're going to have to come back later. I'm just taking care of the children, and I don't know anything about the stero."

A short time later the kid did come back, and Gary met him on the front porch and said, "Hello. What's up?"

"Well, I hear you're giving away your stereo."

"Where did you hear that?" Gary asked.

"Just around. Somebody said you were giving it away,

and since it's such a nice component system that you have, I'd really be interested if you're wanting to get rid of it."

"Wait a minute." Gary turned around. The stereo could not be seen from the doorway, and he knew it was not visible from the street. "Now wait a minute. How did you know it was a component system?"

"Well. . . ."

"How did you know it wasn't a portable or a console? How did you know it was a component system? You were one of the guys in here, weren't you? You were one of the guys in my house the other day!"

"Well . . . yeah."

"You came back because you were in here and you wanted me to know, didn't you?"

"Well . . . I didn't plan to tell you, but I just had to come back."

"I'm not mad that you broke into my house, but that's really serious." Gary stood, just staring at him. "I'm not mad that you stole some of the stuff. I'm not mad that you. . . ."

"Well, what are you mad about then?" the kid asked.

Gary stopped for a moment, chuckled, and said, "Yeah. I guess I am mad about that."

In an attempt to respond as a Christian, he'd been denying the feelings that were natural for being violated in such a random way.

They chatted for a while longer. The kid was from Cleveland and was in town for the summer, living with his aunt and uncle. He apologized for breaking into Gary's house. Apparently he had done it because of the influence of the other gang members and basically wanted to get back with his family before something more happened to him.

7
Prosecution

The April evening was one of the first warm evenings of the year. The winter storm windows had not yet been exchanged for summer screens, so Mary Anne Berry opened both the main windows and the storm windows a few inches to admit the breeze. Then she went to bed, leaving the lights on, expecting her husband to arrive home from his evening meeting within a short time.

She dozed off but awakened to hear footsteps in the hall. At first she thought the sounds were those of her husband, Bill, but then she realized that they were heavier and more hurried. She opened the bedroom door into the hall a crack and looked out just as a tall black man passed her door again with the same hurried steps. Mary Anne was sure then that he was stealing the stereo. That was the only thing of value that he could be taking from the living room. She remembered that Bill had once said that the only thing he'd really mind having stolen was the stereo. He was sure he'd miss that and, with the limited common budget we live on in the Fellowship, it would be difficult to replace it.

Now, am I going to stand here and let this man walk out of here with the stereo? she thought. Then she remembered

the experience of Joan Vogt and the way she had challenged
some thieves and they had dropped what they were stealing.
So she took a deep breath, opened the door, and shouted
after him. "Where are you going with that?"

By that time the intruder was on his way out the kitchen
door, so Mary Anne ran behind him, slammed the door, and
locked it. Then she dialed 911 to call the police. She told
them by phone what had happened and gave them a
description of the man whom she had seen clearly and
closely as he had walked down the hall.

The police arrived within two or three minutes. A second
squad car simultaneously blocked off the exit from their one-
way street and stopped a car with a man in it who fit the
general description Mary Anne had given over the phone.
However, the police officer did not think he had enough information to hold the man, so after taking down some notes,
including the car's license plate number, the officer released
the man.

However, after Mary Anne gave a fuller account of what
had happened and what the man looked like, the police decided that the man they had stopped at the end of the street
was probably the thief. They sent out a call, and another
squad car located the man and stopped him again. At that
time he had a girlfriend with him in the car. The girl
claimed that she had been with the man all evening and the
reason she had not been seen when the police stopped the
man the first time was that she had been lying down.

Then, instead of arranging a line-up from which Mary
Anne would have to identify the person she'd seen in her
house from others, the police brought the man back to the
house and asked Mary Anne if he was the man. She had no
doubt that he was and said so, but that slip weakened the
prosecution and could have endangered Mary Anne if he

had been the wrong person. (The man was wanted on some other charges, and could have sought revenge for Mary Anne's role in having him picked up.)

After the positive identification, the police searched the alley and found all the stereo components neatly placed in a secluded place down the alley. However, they did not check fingerprints on the stereo or in the house or on the windows which the thief had raised to gain entrance. The police took the equipment to the station and impounded it as evidence until the case was closed, during which time the Berrys were denied its use.

After consulting with others, Bill and Mary Anne decided to prosecute. The man had come into the house, had stolen the stereo, and Mary Anne had identified him within ten minutes of the incident.

However, the court process was so slow and delayed so often the situation seemed hopeless. At one point Mary Anne had the idealistic notion that some conciliatory sentence could be suggested. Perhaps the court would tell the defendant to meet with the Berrys a series of times so that they could learn to know and hopefully trust each other, or possibly some other constructive sentence. She mentioned the idea to the state's attorney, and he nearly laughed Mary Anne out of the room. "There's no way you could recommend or influence a sentence," He said. Mary Anne felt embarrassed by the derisive tone of his answer.

The defense attorney made a two-pronged defense. He challenged Mary Anne's ability to identify his client accurately, and he did everything he could to impede the progress of the trial, filing for continuance after continuance. In the end this latter tactic won a dismissal but not until after Mary Anne had to go through a grueling time on the stand in which she felt like *she* was being placed on trial. After she gave a brief description of what happened, the attorney fired question after question at her which seemed to be built on the premise that she would not have noticed anything distinctive about a stranger in her home.

"How could you see this man in the dark? You had been in bed asleep, and it was late at night," he quizzed.

"Look," answered Mary Anne, "he was so close that I could have reached out and touched him. Besides there are six 40-watt bulbs in our dining room that were shining right into his face as well as a light in the bathroom that. . . ." But before she could finish her sentence, the judge cut her off.

That seemed to happen frequently. She didn't feel that she had any freedom or that the court was sympathetic with the fact that she was the one whose home had been invaded and her belongings stolen.

"Is there a man in this courtroom whom you think looks like the man who entered your house?" the defense attorney asked.

"Yes, and he's sitting right there!" Mary Anne said as she pointed at the defendant. She anticipated the next question because she had seen an attorney talking to another man who looked very much like the person who had taken the stereo.

"Is there another person in the courtroom who looks like the defendant?"

"There certainly is," snapped Mary Anne, "and he's sitting right there. . . ." She wanted to go on and say how angry it made her that the attorney was making such an effort to prove that she was confused, but the judge cut her off. Later she learned that the look-alike was the defendant's cousin, and she realized that in one way the defense attorney was just doing his job and pursuing a reasonable path. But it was difficult to be made to feel that she was the one on trial.

Through this whole process a victim/witness advocate was assigned to Mary Anne. And though he could not represent her or accompany her to the stand, he was helpful in explaining each of the events before they happened and he was very supportive.

The case was continued. Bill went on the assigned date and on a following date, but each time there was a further postponement. After that they checked by phone with the court clerk only to find that again and again someone was sick or out of town or for some other reason the date was reassigned until so much time had passed that resolution seemed hopeless.

Finally in November, seven months after the burglary, Bill and Mary Anne decided that they would prefer to have their stereo back rather than continue the hassle or take more time off work to go fruitlessly to court. They phoned the state's attorney's office and said that they would like to drop the charges. They signed some papers and picked up their stereo equipment. It needed some repair for damage it had sustained in the ordeal, but this was the end of the experience for them.

8
Reflections II: Deterrents

When the police speak to civic groups about how crime can be prevented they sometimes emphasize such things as better locks, engraving your name on all valuables, and recording the serial numbers so that if they are stolen and recovered you can identify which things belong to you. They emphasize better lighting on the streets and more money for their department so that they can increase their staff, receive further training, and improve their equipment. Our Evanston Police have been saying that they desperately need to improve their records system by putting everything on computer so that in a matter of moments from the time an officer calls in about someone he has stopped, he can have all the information necessary for making a sound arrest.

All of these things may be valuable and have their place in dealing with crime, but we have discovered a few deterrents to add to the list which are not likely to appear in the little pamphlets the police hand out after their talk.

1. *Reduced possessions.* As a church we have felt called to try to live responsibly in the context of worldwide resources and needs. For many of us this has meant a reduction or limitation on our possessions. Our homes often lack the

items which attract thieves. We try to repair rather than replace. We make our own items when possible, and when we buy new things, we shop for durability rather than high class. Our dressers do not have boxes of valuable jewelry on them. Our tablewear is seldom silver and crystal. Our closets don't have furs hanging in them. In fact, our clothes and furnishings are often secondhand. We try not to be drab, but simple.

We even anticipated that when we began having nice stereos in our homes, they would become a frequent target for thieves—and that's been the case. But for the most part, a burglar would not be able to fence or resell the things he'd find in our homes.

This approach to crime prevention should not be underestimated. In the short run it may appear that it serves only us, that a determined thief would pick on our neighbors if they have more valuable possessions. In certain instances that may be true, but in the long run it means that our whole neighborhood is less enticing, and that does serve everyone. Also, a reduction in burglaries means a reduction in the accompanying crimes—assault, shootings, drug dependence, and the like.

2. *Close proximity.* When the psalmist David wrote, "Behold, how good and how pleasant it is for brethren to dwell together in unity!" (Psalm 133:1, KJV), he was probably thinking about security as well as all the other benefits, because that is a significant one. Even the police say that nothing helps prevent crime better than nosy neighbors. But the sad fact is that most people prefer their privacy so much that they often know little about their neighbors closest to them, let alone the other people on the block.

The kind of knowledge we have of one another in our church is similar to that which exists in small towns. We live close. We know each other's schedules and when people should be home or not. We know when a member has guests or relatives visiting which make it legitimate for strangers to be going in and out of their home, and usually the visitors are soon introduced. We freely and frequently enter each other's homes, thereby becoming familiar with what's normal and even which items should not be seen under someone else's arm as they walk down the street. When we are in our neighborhood, we are almost always within calling distance of someone we know and trust.

Many of us live in extended-family households. These were designed for ministry and fellowship, but because they include several adults, someone is almost always home, and usually more than one person is in the house. Even in our apartment buildings, families who live across the hall from each other often leave their doors open for friendly interaction. This kind of living brings better security than any lock, electronic gadget, guard dog, or weapon.

And it has its benefits for our neighbors too. A spirit of awareness and cohesiveness develops on the streets. Because we stay in the neighborhood and intimately know as many people as we do, we tend to know many of the rest of our neighbors. If we don't know them by name, we know them by sight and that they live next door to so and so.

The other day Walt Jones noticed a couple of strange men cruising slowly down the street looking carefully both ways at everything they passed. Walt stepped out beside their car and said, "Hi. You're not from this neighborhood, are you? Can I help you?" They stammered, "No," and drove off at a normal speed, looking at the street ahead of them instead of in everybody's window. Maybe they had nothing illegal in mind, but if they had, Walt blew their anonymity.

3. *Reconciliation and God's peace.* In spite of the public's

fear of criminals, most violent crimes occur between ac-
quaintances, often family members. They are the result of
long-standing resentments, smoldering feuds, explosive
tempers, too much drinking, marital strife, and the frustration of not knowing how to cope with raising children. Those
are the situations into which the church can bring good
news, but too often it doesn't, and people are left with their
tensions until they explode.

In Romans 12:18 Paul says, "So far as it depends upon
you, live peaceably with all." That requires us to learn and
employ the skills of communication and reconciliation in
order to bring God's understanding, forgiveness, and peace
to one another before anyone needs to ask whether the
police should be called.

It is the kind of deterrent that caused the judge to direct
Josie and Ern to get marital counseling from the Fellowship
instead of sending Ern to jail. It is the kind of courage to in-
quire of your neighbors if something seems to be going on
that shouldn't. It is learning how to ask someone else to turn
down the music without insulting him instead of waiting
until you are so angry that you cannot speak in a friendly
manner.

But this takes skill. Sometimes our ability to bring real
peace is so inadequate that we cannot call it true reconciliation, but perhaps we can head off greater violence.

For instance, one night as I left the house, some of the
most angry yelling I've ever heard seemed to be coming
from just around the corner. The ruckus had been escalating
for several minutes before I'd come out the door. I hurried to
see what was happening. When I got to the corner, I saw
four black men and one black woman yelling at a white man
in a car stopped in the middle of the street. The man in the
car was yelling back at the others loud enough to match

them all, calling them names and especially degrading the woman. I thought he must be crazy.

At first I hung back, not seeing the cause of the harangue or anything I could do about it. Then the guy in the car stepped on the gas, squealed around the corner and halfway down the next block where he stopped with a screech. He put his car in reverse and came racing backwards down the street, fishtailing around the corner, nearly hitting the people standing in the street before he stopped. That was too much. They'd had it. They didn't stop with jumping for the safety of the curb. They ran across the sidewalk and started pulling up some steel fence posts that didn't have any fencing attached to them.

Unable to think of anything else, I ran up to the guy's car, looked in the window, and said, "What are you doing? Do you live around here?" The guy shook his head. "Then get out of here!" I said. He looked at me like he couldn't believe that I'd said what I'd said, so I pointed down the street and yelled with all my might, "I said, get out of here!"

He put his car into gear and tore away. When I turned around I didn't know whether I'd face those other guys with their steel posts or not. Fortunately, they kept their threats and rage focused on the receding taillights. A few moments later as I started to walk away, one of them said, "Hey, thanks."

Maybe this was too crude to be called God's peace, and it certainly didn't accomplish reconciliation, but maybe it prevented something worse.

9
Christian Landlords

"Buy two apartment buildings and become landlords? That's the craziest idea I've heard anyone propose for the Fellowship."

And I thought I knew why it didn't make sense. To be the landlord to many people was to be their enemy; nothing else was possible. The only experience I'd had in managing rental property was as coordinator for an urban educational program located on the South Side of Chicago. The program was designed to allow students from suburban colleges to do short-term study in the city. We rented a large, old church in Hyde Park. Our program operated out of the educational wing of the building, and we tried to sublet the auditorium to different groups so that we could recoup some of the expense for the large building.

It never worked. We were trying to operate on a shoestring, unable to invest the money and time needed to maintain a suitable public auditorium. Our worst failure was with a well-known black playwright and musician. He had just returned to his home in Chicago from New York after an extended, Off-Broadway run of his latest musical.

He decided he wanted to stage the musical on the South

Side. "The Church" suited his needs ... and his nearly empty pocketbook. From the beginning there was trouble, big trouble. His crew wanted to build a stage, so we arrived at an imprecise agreement of what could be altered. But before we knew it, the console of the old pipe organ was taken out with an ax, as was the altar rail and several other pieces of furniture. Also the pulpit was painted orange to be used as one of the props in the play.

We should have ended the arrangement right then, but with our foolish liberal hearts (in need of the rent money and afraid of being called racist) we went on with the plan.

Things went downhill from there. One night when the furnace wouldn't work there was a near riot, and frequently our sleep was interrupted in the middle of the night by someone who had left something inside of the building and needed to have it right then. Once someone even pulled a gun and started waving it around.

The play didn't do well in Chicago, and the theater group got behind on the rent. In the middle of winter we didn't have enough money to buy the hundreds of gallons of fuel it took to heat the place each week. Finally, the show closed before we pursued a legal eviction.

It was one of the worst experiences of my life, and I didn't want to see Reba Place get involved in being landlords. Apartment managing might be different from renting to a low-budget but militant theater group, especially if the manager took good care of the buildings, but I didn't know many tenants who had any love for their landlords. If we wanted to relate to our black neighbors, buying apartment buildings seemed to be about as wise as singing "Dixie."

On the other hand, the two buildings we were considering were the worst buildings in our neighborhood. The owner was in trouble with the city because the 44 units had a total of 160 Building Code violations (some of them serious) listed against them. Fellowship houses surrounded the buildings, and we anticipated having some Fellowship members live right in the buildings. We certainly wouldn't be absentee landlords, and we had a skilled construction crew that would be capable of putting the buildings in shape.

Finally, it seemed that God wanted us to try the venture in spite of the obstacles. Still, what would we do if people fell behind in paying their rent? Would we have the sheriff evict them? Would people take advantage of us when they realized that we weren't quick to take them to court?

Six years have passed since we purchased those two buildings. All of the apartments were quickly brought up to code. Then we set about remodeling the apartments—sanding and revarnishing the floors, painting the walls, rebuilding the kitchens and bathrooms. One of the first things we did was to lay new sod outside and plant flowers. At first the yards were hard to maintain, but now they are some of the nicest apartment yards in the neighborhood.

Our relations with the tenants have gone well also. Many of us live in the buildings too. However, we have limited our occupancy to about 40 percent of the apartments so that they don't become all-Fellowship buildings. Two years ago we purchased another 22-unit building a block away so that we could continue the service in the same way.

In all of this time there have been only two evictions, and neither of those required any legal action. One eviction involved a tenant who seemed to be dealing quite extensively in drugs and creating a bad influence in the building. The other one happened much more reluctantly. It involved a woman on welfare with four children under the age of ten. There are other tenants on welfare, but this woman consistently couldn't manage her money, and she kept falling further and further behind in her rent over a period of two and a half years. During that time Matthew Roddy, our apartment manager, tried a variety of approaches to help her with her budgeting. Finally, it seemed clear that continuing the arrangement was just perpetuating her irresponsibility and sometimes dishonesty. Knowing that it would be hard for her to find another place, Matthew reluctantly told her that she would have to move, and we prayed that God would provide some better solution.

At the last moment she was notified that she had been approved for a new, federally subsidized town house. The fact that she was being evicted had bounced her name to the top of a waiting list that might have otherwise taken years. The new apartment costs her only $70 per month, a rental fee far easier for her to manage. We were able to help her move. Several months later she wrote Matthew a letter thanking him for his patience with her for so long and affirming that asking her to move had not only been fair but had proved to be helpful. She also noted that she had started attending a nearby church with her children.

Rent collection has not produced nearly as many problems as we anticipated. At this point only about four tenants are behind on their rent for a total of $1,500, but in each case arrangements have been worked out so they can gradually catch up. In the last two years only $830 has been lost as "unrecoverable rent," a small fraction of the rental loss managers usually expect.

What makes the difference? Our personal involvement shows that we care. We live with and around our tenants. Matthew is always there. He will help people install a fancy light fixture, offer suggestions on decorating, and try to work things out if there are problems. Sometimes that has even included helping people with budget planning.

In terms of rent, the legal route that is sometimes followed by management agencies is much more expensive than the personal approach. By the time a person gets far enough behind that some action is necessary, a couple months' rent has been lost. In addition about $300 in court fees are needed to pursue an eviction, plus lawyer's fees. It usually takes at least two months before an eviction is served, and during that time many tenants who know they are going to be evicted will make no further effort to pay. Before the mess is over, an eviction can cost the equivalent of half-a-year's rent in totally unrecoverable monies, as well as a lot of ill-will and pain.

But Matthew expresses far more than a concern for collecting the rent and protecting the property. In a recent example one of the tenants called Matthew (not the police) because she thought she heard another tenant beating one of his children. Matthew went up to check, but he didn't go without apprehension. Matthew is white, and he knew that this particular tenant was black and did not like white people.

When Matthew knocked on the door, he asked to talk to the father. The man was angry at first, especially as Matthew explained that he had come because of the yelling and just wanted to make sure no one was getting hurt.

"It's just my kid, none of your business," the man said.

"I know you love your kids, but sometimes when people get upset they do things they later regret."

"He's okay. Come on out here and show the man you're okay."

The boy came out and indeed seemed to be unharmed. Apparently there had been a lot more yelling than action.

Matthew started to leave. "I can see that he's okay. I'm sorry for bothering you. I hope you aren't angry at me. I feel supportive of your role as a father."

"That's okay. That's okay. You don't need to apologize. Actually I appreciate your concern. I know that people do abuse their children sometimes, and not many people would get involved."

"Yeah, I guess that's true. Most people just mind their own business," Matthew said.

"Yeah. Well, you know, I guess I was pretty angry with the kid, almost out of control, now that I think about it. But he makes me so mad. He's only ten years old, and he's already running around with older dudes and messing with dope."

The man went on to explain many of his frustrations and concerns about raising kids in the city. Then he thanked Matthew for coming up. "You know, you folks are different. I know that you respect people."

10
Vandalism

To live in the city is to live with vandalism. The problem seems more prevalent because the higher density of people brings a greater concentration of all human problems. But crowding itself seems to generate hostilities which often find their expression in the destruction of property.

And beyond this, many destructive or irresponsible acts have more serious consequences in the city. In the country, the kid who chops down a tree just for the fun of it may not have his deed noticed any more than if he spends the afternoon throwing rocks. But if he tries either activity in the city, he'll soon have someone angry at him. And where can he build a fire, shoot a sling shot, or whittle with a knife in peace in the city?

When I was a kid living in the country I dug caves and traps, threw homemade boomerangs, and broke the windows and lights out of old car bodies placed along the riverbank to stop erosion. I mixed my own black powder and built a cannon which could put a slug the size of a thumb through a six-inch cedar post. I learned to drive on old dirt roads and rebuilt cars from the time I was 16. Sometimes I'd slip off to run one through the quarter-mile "drag strip" marked off on a straight piece of highway where the traffic was slight.

Yet, I think that my folks would say that I was a reasonably cooperative and responsible kid, and I sure didn't count myself among the wilder kids in my high school.

Normal or not, many of those activities could have been serious in a city. Maybe I would have had sense enough not to do them where it was unsafe; I don't know.

A few weeks ago I discovered that my ten-year-old son, Julian, and some of his friends had found a loose panel on the door of our neighbor's unused garage. The kids had turned the place into a clubhouse, complete with old chairs, a rug, candles, and a membership list written on the wall. I strongly reprimanded the kids for going into someone else's place without permission, for messing it up, and especially for the candle and the danger of fire in the city. I made them move their things out, clean up, and apologize to the owner. But I shielded the kids from some of his anger because I had sympathy for the idea of turning an abandoned place into a clubhouse. I remembered doing exactly the same thing when I was ten years old. I had also gotten in trouble because my name had been written on the "membership list" on the wall of somebody else's unused building.

That kind of behavior needs discipline whether it happens in the city, a small town, or the country. But somehow when it happens in the city it adds to that long list of emotionally overwhelming events about which many people, like our neighbor, feel helpless and angry. Maybe the feelings are aggravated by the impersonal nature of the city. The victim experiences the damage, hears stories of what has happened to other people, but seldom knows whether the trouble-causers are caught. And even when the victim learns that the vandals have been caught, he seldom knows them or hears how they turn out in years to come. Do they become serious criminals or solid citizens? The victim's impression is that the world is getting worse and worse, and maybe it is. However, the primary cause of the overwhelmed feelings is not an objective analysis but a growing list of unresolved violations which he has experienced.

Some time ago we had our garage set up as a game room for a couple of junior high boys who lived with their mother in our Branch household. One morning we went out to find that the garage had been broken into. The chairs were torn apart, lights were broken, dirt had been poured onto the old pool table, a hole had been knocked into the wall, and records were scattered all around.

I started asking around the neighborhood until I discovered who was responsible—three girls intent on getting revenge for something the boys had done. When I found the girls, their response was hostile. They were streetwise and didn't think there was anything I could do since there was no proof that they had done the damage. But instead of going to the police or trying to prove that I had some kind of power, I talked to their mothers.

One of the mothers demonstrated why her daughter was so defiant. She set the example; she didn't care what her child had done. She said I had no business bothering her about the problem. But the other two mothers were deeply concerned. In each case they called their daughter in, and we all talked. I went away feeling there was a good chance that some kind of useful correction had happened. In the process I got to know the girls and was able to greet them by name on the street after that.

But that was a lot of trouble. In fact, coping with vandalism seems always to demand a lot. For instance, it means the removal of things which invite vandalism. Recently we had finished installing some nice glass bricks in the alley windows of our meetinghouse. Three of them were broken out only days later. The glass is thick and could not have been broken by the pebbles normally found in the alley, but a little investigation showed that the windows had been broken by bricks, the red bricks that our workman had taken out of the wall and left on the ground to be cleaned up later.

In our neighborhood anyone who leaves a disabled car on the street for more than a few days invites its stripping or destruction. If you don't pick up the loose curb stones or broken pieces of sidewalk in front of your house, someone else may do the job for you and deposit them on the front seat of your car—through the windshield. Graffiti left on anything begins a contest.

It's easy to become cynical. Why should freedom from crime depend upon how vigilantly one can guard against those who are just waiting for an opportunity to destroy something or harass someone? It puts the Christian to the test of being long-suffering, dealing with anger, and resisting prejudice.

A few summers ago a gang of teenagers commandeered the front porch of a building two doors down from us. None of the kids lived there, but often as many as 20 gathered on the steps playing their radios and jiving around until the early hours of the morning. The residents of the building were afraid and unable to do anything. The front of the building was severely vandalized and the yard and hedges trampled. The new paint was grayed by dirty hands and soon chipped and written on. A bike locked on the porch was torn apart and destroyed. Other items were stolen. Always trash and cans were thrown around when they were there.

The kids insulted and intimidated passersby and sometimes refused to move so the people who lived in the building could go up their own steps. The kids threatened to cut or shoot anyone who would mess with them. Most of it was just talk, but they keyed each other up and dared each other into behavior that could have been serious. This was especially true when the girls would taunt the guys with comments like: "Are you going to let that man tell you what to do?" when someone would try to speak to them about their behavior.

One Saturday, after a lot of abuse to one of the residents of the building, the police came. I thought the man had called the police himself, but he disappeared into his apartment, possibly not wanting to be identified as the caller. The kids scattered the moment the police came around the corner. I finally went over to talk to the police.

When the police left, the kids quickly regrouped. They thought I'd called the police and immediately began declaring how they were going to get even by bricking our windows or something.

Later in the afternoon when a few of the folks from our household were sitting out in the backyard and my daughter, who was two years old at the time, was running around, a barrage of a half dozen stones crashed around us. Another brother and I ran down the alley to try and catch the kids. All but a couple ran off before we got there. I grabbed the biggest one and backed him up to the fence and began to give him the verbal third degree to force him to identify who threw the stones. He wouldn't tell.

That night I felt depressed. I was shocked by the fantasy scenarios going through my mind. My fantasies didn't involve plans to call the police or organize the neighborhood or contact the parents. I wanted to crack some heads. Those kids became the "enemy," and I distanced myself from them. At every idle moment my mind drifted back to the afternoon and the rage I wanted to vent. I was hooked.

Finally, I confessed to the Lord how totally I was failing in an area I deeply wanted to follow Him, in loving my offender and working for neighborhood peace. I felt like an utter fool. My pride was injured. I hadn't taught those kids a lesson on their own terms, and I hadn't shown them any reflection of God's kingdom either.

Such experiences are like homework and show me how far I am by nature from being a peaceful person. Some people may find it easy to respond more calmly, but not me. I must rely again and again on the Lord's grace and forgiveness which accepts me just the way I am, then leads me to desire to change and to grow.

11
Police State

In 1968 I made my decision to seek a discharge from the military as a conscientious objector. Ironically, it was not because I had personally been involved in the gore of a foreign combat like the Vietnam War as so many of my contemporaries had. Instead, my convictions grew out of my engagement in urban "police actions" as a member of the National Guard. The relevance of that experience to this discussion is that there are times when the police relate to people like an army relates to its enemies.

In most secular situations, survival supersedes moral restraint. When a society, a police force, or even an individual policeman feels seriously threatened, civil rights can be forgotten. The better trained and disciplined the police are, the more tolerance they may have developed. But anytime we call upon the police, who are prepared to use lethal force when necessary, we must remember that their response is out of our control. And it can include that ugly end of the spectrum which I experienced while in the National Guard—be it a single policeman pushed beyond his limit or a frightened city.

After Dr. Martin Luther King, Jr., was assassinated in the

spring of 1968, many areas of Chicago were torn by riots. My National Guard unit, which was normally stationed 30 miles away in Elgin, was assigned to the blocks immediately around the storefront building of the black church of which I was a member.

That afternoon I did not come chugging up in my little green VW. I went rumbling by in the back of a two-and-a-half-ton army truck bristling with weapons. I did not call out friendly hellos when I saw someone I knew on the street. I pulled my helmet low over my eyes and wondered what I was doing.

When our convoy turned onto Roosevelt Road the smoke was so thick that it was hard to see a block. The street was laced with fire hoses. Familiar stores were blazing infernos. People were running everywhere.

On a side street we drove past the homes of people I knew, children I taught in Sunday school. "Damn niggers. Why don't they behave themselves," one of my army buddies said. He was speaking about everyone not wearing a green or blue police helmet. Those "niggers" were his enemy, making him miss his work and family. They were even threatening the life he knew.

"Hey nigger bitch, what do you got for us?" another guy yelled as we passed a couple girls sitting on their stoop.

Later in the afternoon, when the fires were starting to subside, we were deployed on various street corners as support for the police. The press and various civic leaders were commending the restraint of the law enforcement people, but Mayor Daley was worried about what would happen when the night came. "Get tougher," he ordered. "Shoot to kill arsonists and shoot to maim looters."

Just before dark one of the cars approaching our road-blocked intersection made a sudden U-turn 50 yards before it got there and headed back the other way. The police opened fire. The car didn't stop. Fortunately, none of the people on the sidewalks were hit by stray bullets.

The police didn't follow the car. There were no obvious grounds for an arrest. The car *might* have contained looters with their stolen goods. Or it *might* have contained people who were just turning around because they saw they couldn't get through on that street. But society was in danger. Evidence of a crime was not necessary. Due process was waived. Civil rights were ignored, and people were deliberately shot at.

A couple nights later a squad of us were sent down a dark alley to check out the rumor of a sniper. We were scared. He could have been anywhere, ready to pick one of us off before we could dive behind a telephone pole or a junked car. "Hold it," someone whispered. "There was a noise up that fire escape."

We all took cover and squinted in the dark. There was a movement, and the lieutenant in front of me aimed at it. A light in the window flipped on, and a child drew back his head. "What you doin' out of bed?" a woman yelled.

We stumbled back out of the alley and returned to our posts guarding the remaining stores. A few days later we rolled up our sleeping bags, gathered our dirty uniforms, and went home.

That was April. In August I was back on the streets of Chicago, again facing people I knew with my weapon and the threat of death. The occasion was the 1968 National Democratic Convention. This time I wasn't assigned to a familiar neighborhood and actually only saw two or three people I knew, but what I saw happen to the police was even more revealing of the effect of threat on those in power.

For months the pressure had been building. National outrage over the Vietnam War was probably the largest factor. People were determined that their voice, which had been ignored for so many years, would be heard as election time neared. But there were also the yippies, hippies, thugs, and cynics who took advantage of the opportunity to disrupt the city and thumb their noses at society. The Chicago Police had reason to be worried. By Wednesday, August 18, 10,000 demonstrators had gathered in Lincoln Park on Chicago's near North Side. The 12,000-man police force requested the help of 5,000 National Guardsmen. At first we were kept in reserve, housed in armories and in park field houses around the city.

The confrontations began. We read about them in the papers or watched them on portable TV's that some of the men had managed to bring along. Rally and march permits that had been granted were at first restricted and then revoked. The radicals made the most of that as proof that basic American freedoms had been replaced by a "fascist regime" intent on ignoring the people and on continuing its war by whatever means necessary.

On Monday 6,000 Army troops were airlifted to the Chicago area to stand in reserve. They were equipped with full field gear, including rifles, flame throwers, and bazookas. There were also hundreds of Secret Service, FBI, sheriffs, and state police. In all about 24,000 armed men were on duty in Chicago—a sizable army.

The confrontations between the police and the demonstrators turned ugly. In the parks, on the streets, and in many situations the police proved vulnerable to the verbal taunting of the more obscene demonstrators. The demonstrators attacked the police, spit on them, and threw dangerous objects. Soon the police were exhausted, angry, and worried. Reports began coming in of police attacking people. Members of the press seemed to be prime targets; the police did not like them recording their actions on tape or film.

Finally, after days of violence, our Guard unit, the Second Battalion of the 129th Infantry, was called upon for the day and night that proved to be the most serious—Wednesday, the 28th, when the Democratic presidential candidate was to be nominated. Shortly after noon we took up positions south of the Field Museum. We were to be in position if the police could not control a large rally that was beginning in the Grant Park band shell area just north of the museum, and we were to prevent any demonstrators from marching south and southwest where they might approach the Amphitheatre in which the convention was being held.

As the rally dragged on through the afternoon, the Secret Service estimated the crowd's size at about 10,000, and there were reports that some of the demonstrators (possibly 100) were armed with sticks, rocks, bottles, and other weapons. Small incidents flared throughout the afternoon which heated up the crowd's fury. Some were said to have been started by police provocateurs.

At about 4:30 in the afternoon a large fracas erupted when a unit of policemen charged into the crowd swinging their batons and bloodying several heads. They later claimed that they were trying to arrest someone who had lowered the American flag from a pole and replaced it with a red rag.

For a few minutes order seemed to prevail as the speakers urged the crowd to remain calm and nonviolent. Then about 100 policemen lined up and waded into the crowd. At first they marched forward in a disciplined fashion, but then they broke ranks and clubbed anyone they could hit.

Fearing that the crowd would march west over some

bridges, into the Loop, and on to the Amphitheatre, our company was loaded on trucks and driven around where we were redeployed to guard the bridges at Balbo Drive and the Congress Plaza. The area at both bridges was extremely wide and we had only enough men to stand at about an arm's length from each other. Our orders were to allow individuals through our lines but not groups that might appear to constitute an organized march. We also had to allow vehicles through. The next bridge north of us was open. No attempt was made to close it. This meant that with the south and west sides of the park closed off and the lake to the east, the only exit was to the north. Anyone wanting to go west, first had to go far enough north to find an open bridge.

At Balbo our men set up two machine guns. I have no idea who gave that order or what the person thought would be done with machine guns. Would the U.S. Army have actually opened fire with machine guns on a crowd of U.S. citizens who insisted on crossing the first bridge instead of going north to the third bridge which was open?

I was among those blocking the second bridge at Congress. I was assigned to carry a radio on my back that day. That meant that I was armed with a pistol instead of a rifle. With my free hand I operated my camera. I later turned over some of the pictures to the President's National Commission on the Causes and Prevention of Violence.

The demonstrators had organized themselves into a column in an area of the park out of our sight. For nearly an hour the leaders tried again to obtain permission for a march. As the time passed, some people broke off from the group and drifted over to the bridges we were blocking. Because they came as individuals, we let them through. Joined by others, they began regrouping behind us in the Loop area. Before long there was a crowd of 2,000 behind us and still another 5,000 in front of us.

At about 6:00 p.m. efforts to obtain a permit were abandoned, and the march column began to disperse. However, because it was out of our sight, we did not know this. We were expecting to have to stop a "march." Instead, we began getting larger and larger numbers of "individuals" which we let through, until finally someone gave the order to close the bridge to anyone who looked like a demonstrator. That created real tension. We had let some people through; suddenly, without explanation, we stopped others. As the crowd began to build up in front of us, those who had gone through came back from behind to heckle and push us. Our ranks were too thin, and as we shifted to one side to take care of a disturbance, people would dart through the widened gaps down the line.

By this time the flow of business people and office workers on their way home was at its peak. Many had cars parked east of the bridge. In the park a baseball game concluded. Players in their uniforms and families with their picnic baskets began to join the crowd in front of us. They wanted to cross the bridge to get to the trains and buses that would take them home. Discriminating between demonstrators and other people was impossible. In fact, most demonstrators were not hippies or distinguishable from any other citizen.

Finally, we received the word to close the bridge entirely, except for vehicles. Nobody thought about them. A traffic jam was building in front of us and behind us. The cacophony of horns and the yelling, chanting crowd was deafening. The cars nudged forward until we parted to let them through. Inevitably, a couple of demonstrators would break through at the same time. Occasionally, some would leap on top of the cars and run across as the crowd whooped and cheered. It was an angry game of taunts and dares.

As soon as it was obvious that we were letting cars through, drivers would open their doors, fill their cars with demonstrators, and try to transport them through our lines.

Many Guardsmen were getting angry at being made to look like impotent buffoons. But what could they do? They were too outnumbered to scuffle back in kind and hold their line. Should they shoot, stab a few people with bayonets, or crush some faces with rifle butts?

Some police showed up swinging their long riot clubs, and they had no hesitation about using them. They wore sweaters, which covered their nametags and numbers, making it impossible to identify them except by photograph. They beat anyone who couldn't get out of their way. One man was struck to the ground near me by several blows. His head was a bloody mess, but he was not arrested. No one had seen him do anything wrong. He had just been one of the first to fall when the police came through. And then the police were gone as fast as they had come.

Finally the Guard uncorked its tear gas. Several canisters were thrown, and a man with a converted flamethrower walked up and down our line spraying an enormous cloud. Several demonstrators were gassed right in the face. He came to a red Corvair into which some badly gassed demonstrators had climbed, hoping the woman driver would get them through the line. When the demonstrators didn't get out immediately, the Guardsman pumped the car full of tear gas at point-blank range.

Choking, coughing, and crying, the crowd began to flee. Many jumped into Buckingham fountain trying to wash the noxious, burning powder off their skin. Finally, the crowd got the information that the next bridge north was completely open and free from gas. The gas was blowing southwest into the Loop, especially into the Conrad Hilton Hotel which housed many of the Convention delegates.

Our vehicles finally came to pick us up and take us to our staging area in the parking lot south of Soldier's Field. There we waited until we were needed again a few hours later. Canteen trucks opened up and many of us were eating our first food since breakfast. We mixed with hundreds of police also waiting in reserve. They were tired; many of them had been on duty 12 to 14 hours, but their anger had not cooled. Most of them were itching to get back into the action. Some of the more boisterous ones were stamping around, shouting, "I wan'a bust some heads! Le' me bust some heads!" Another said, "I'm going to kill one of those God damned hippies tonight, man. You think I'm kidding, but I'm going to kill one!" That kind of talk was everywhere among the police. Some Guardsmen entered in; others were shocked.

While we were off the streets some awful things happened. The crowd had regrouped west of the bridges on Michigan Avenue. It joined the mule train of the SCLC Poor People's Campaign. Ralph Abernathy had a permit for his mule train to be moving south on Michigan Avenue at that time. The eight lanes of the street, the sidewalks, and every available space was packed with the chanting throng. Newsmen, TV cameras, mobile units, and batteries of lights were everywhere. As the crowd moved south, they met a solid police line near the Conrad Hilton. Thousands of people were boxed into a very small area.

The crowd started to bulge west at the intersection of Balbo. A platoon of police sealed off that exit. Some people were becoming frightened of being trapped. Others were sure that the live media coverage would offer protection from the indiscriminate police attacks they had known on previous nights in the parks and streets.

But for some unknown reason the police on Balbo charged. They were reinforced by another platoon. According to films they seemed to grab anyone they could get hold of and beat them. People kept falling over each other and getting trampled. The pressure on the crowd increased the pressure on the south against the police line that was blocking the street. That line of police began chanting, "Push 'em back, push 'em back," and began advancing northward. Periodically the two groups of club-wielding police—those to the south and those to the west—would regroup and charge again into the crowd which had no exit.

On the west side of the street is a narrow park area where the people were supposed to be permitted according to previous police announcements. A number of three-wheeled motorcycles drove up over the curb and into the crowd there, crashing into some people and running over others.

Referring to the TV cameras the crowd began to chant, "The whole world is watching; the whole world is watching." But it made no difference. And by that time the crowd was very ugly, throwing bottles and cans, using sticks from broken benches and whatever else they could grab as weapons. The police chanted back, "Kill, kill, kill!"

A particularly nasty scene occurred when a group of about 150 people were trapped against the Hilton. Most of these people had been bystanders. According to the films, they were there before the crowd moved south down Michigan Avenue. The group included many hotel guests. With their backs against the large plate glass window of the Haymarket Lounge, the people could not move. To the front, the police, who were completely surrounding them on the other three sides, began spraying them with mace and hitting them with their clubs. Finally, the window broke and screaming men and women tumbled through, many severely cut on the jagged edges of glass. A squad of police burst through the door, pursuing them into the bar. They continued to club anyone who looked like a demonstrator or like someone who had fallen through the window, even those who were already too severely wounded to move out of the way.

The worst of the melee lasted for nearly 20 minutes. Finally, the deputy superintendent of police and a few other officials were able to bring a stop to it by pulling their men off demonstrators and shouting, "Stop, damn it, stop! For Christ's sake, stop it!"

Later that evening our unit was loaded up and driven back to the Conrad Hilton to replace the majority of the police. There was a mixture of boos and cheers as we rumbled up. Some feared our addition was preparation for a new assault on the crowd. Some hoped we had come to replace the police and would be less violent.

It was a long and difficult night with plenty of harassment, tension, and several arrests. Again we set up machine guns—maybe it was for a show of force. But there was no more mass violence in front of the Hilton. Instead, it continued on other streets, with smaller groups and away from the cameras.

By 6:00 a.m. the crowd had dwindled to several hundred, most of them sleeping on the grass or sitting around fires that were kept burning in trash baskets. Another Guard unit came to relieve us, and we marched north a block and turned onto the grassy strip. There we too laid down and fell asleep, looking much like the demonstrators except that we all wore green and laid down in straight lines.

On Thursday there was another confrontation as Dick Gregory tried to march with nearly 3,000 people south toward the Amphitheatre. He claimed he was taking them to his house for a party.

By Friday many people who had come to Chicago for the Convention were going home, and things quieted down. During the week 192 policemen were injured; at least 726 civilians were injured, 101 requiring hospitalization. Another 400 were given first aid for severe tear gassing or macing.

As for me, my experiences with the National Guard on the streets of Chicago led me to the Bible, and I finally applied for (and received) a Conscientious Objectors' Discharge from the military. Particularly after my duty around the area of my church, I knew that I could never obey an order to shoot or harm those people. They were my brothers and sisters in the Lord.

Once I acknowledged that fact, I had to ask myself what I would have done if I had been sent to some other part of the city. There I might not have known anyone. It would have been easier to distance myself from the people and think of them as the enemy. If I had been sent to Vietnam, the people might have seemed even more remote. But they wouldn't have been any less human or loved less by God. Actually, what happened to me was that my eyes were opened to the truth of any battlefield. God loved us all and gave His Son to die for us all. As Christians we are never excused from the role of representing that love to every person we meet.

The police do not usually relate to people like they are the enemy. But it can happen. It can happen in situations where the government feels threatened. It can happen when an individual policeman feels threatened. And it can happen with a poorly trained or undisciplined policeman. We must take into account this potential, however remote it might be, whenever we think of using the police.

12
Reflections III: Attitudes

Whether it is God's Law as recorded in the Old Testament or the U.S. Tax Laws, we humans try to find loopholes. That is the reason why Jesus' focus on attitudes was so upsetting to those who heard Him. Jesus was not revealing a harder law but pointing to the intent and spirit of the Law, and that has fewer loopholes. Fidelity and love for one's spouse was the objective of the law against adultery. Therefore, Jesus pointed out that a lustful heart also missed the mark. The same is true about our attitudes toward those whom we might call "enemies."

1. *Love your enemies.* Though Christians in the early church did not participate in killing and warfare, by the beginning of the fifth century, St. Augustine theorized that it was possible to kill one's enemy while still loving him. This paradox was necessary in order to conceive of a "just war," and Augustine was trying to justify war in light of Jesus' command to love one's enemies so that the Roman Empire, then claiming to be Christian, could defend itself. To do this, Augustine reasoned that death was more merciful than allowing an enemy to continue in sin. Of course, the state's cause had to be pure and the enemy's utterly evil so that the

enemy could be seen as sinning and in need of being "rescued." In this way, killing could be considered a loving act while at the same time the state could be defended.

Giving war such a religious justification inevitably led to the Crusades, the Inquisition, and the genocide of many pagans—not because those campaigns met all of Augustine's proposed conditions for waging a "just war," but because such a how-far-can-one-go? approach to morality always leads to gross perversion. It is a kind of legalism which thrives because of its loopholes, and it is the opposite of the spirit which asks, "How close to God's ways can I live?"

It is easier to respect someone who resorts to violence out of desperation and then admits his weakness, than it is to respect the twisted claim that killing is love to the enemy.

Today the theological overtones have largely evaporated, but there are still people who console themselves with the idea that they have no malice toward their enemies, even though they are ready to kill them or lock them in prison. And in our sterile world it is easy to maintain that perspective; we don't have to look inside the prisons and watch what happens from day to day. We don't have to see how hard it is to make a new life upon release.

But when we face violence and crime, it is important for us to examine our attitudes and motives. Do we call the police because we think that that is the most loving thing to do? Is there any cause to think our enemy will benefit? Are we being rational? Or are our theories as absurd as the notion that you can love someone by killing the person? If we can expect the police to be responsible and restrained, the judicial system to be fair, and the penal system to be humane, we might be able to say that calling the police is best for everyone concerned. But it is all too easy to say that we are being loving when there is nothing even remotely loving about the outcome of our actions. We may be covering up a desire for vengeance or the fact that we are too lazy to take the time to relate to an offender in a more personal way.

In this connection it is important to note that a decision *not* to call the police does not prove a person's love either. That too may be a decision motivated by laziness and irresponsibility, or a desire to avoid the pain, or a prideful, idealistic legalism which does not show love.

2. *Trust the spirit of peace within.* Several years ago when I was trying to work out my convictions about peace and reconciliation, I used to construct scenario after scenario of hypothetical, violent situations, trying to figure out what I *should* do. Imaginary scenarios, or better yet, true experiences such as those reported in this book, are useful in training our minds, but they don't build for us a code of conduct. The fact that we've heard that somebody successfully said, "In the name of Jesus, drop your gun," doesn't necessarily mean that we should try the same thing. Neither does the fact that someone else called the police mean we should do that. What we need to develop is a confidence that because we are committed to the peace of Christ and the expression of His love, His Holy Spirit will be able to guide us in the crisis.

I think this became most evident to me as I reviewed my response to the robbery mentioned in the first chapter of this book. I had no formula in mind which said that if one were holding a knife in my face, I could grab his (or her) arm, throw the person to the floor, and wrestle it away. If you'd have asked my opinion before the incident, I'd probably have said that such a response was too dangerous. Certainly if Vicki or one of the other women being robbed had tried it, it might have proved too dangerous. I think they listened to the Lord by cooperating with the robber. Possibly because of my deep commitment not to hurt anyone, the Lord could guide me to take such swift and physical action. Someone else who was internally primed to take an eye for an eye or kill rather than be killed may have been too violent. The difference is in the attitude. My actions could have led to an injury (and we must always evaluate such danger in its own right), but it would have been the result of an honest accident, not the result of an ultimatum.

3. *Respect less violence as well as nonviolence.* We should be grateful and encourage any person in power who restrains himself in a crisis, especially when that restraint comes from a desire for peace and a concern for the welfare of everyone, even the offender. Sometimes we forget this perspective when thinking of the police because we know that they would be willing to use violence, but there can be a lot of difference in the ways police conduct themselves.

Recently the Evanston Police arrested 11 suspected Puerto Rican FALN members. This terrorist organization has claimed responsibility for over 100 bombings across the country which have killed five people and injured 70 others. F-A-L-N, standing for the Fuerzas Armadas de Liberacion Nacional (Armed Forces of National Liberation), identifies a group of leftist Puerto Rican nationalists dedicated to the unconditional independence for the island and freedom for persons it considers political prisoners.

The arrest of the 11 suspected terrorists, which included Carlos Torres (Number One on the FBI's most-wanted list) and his wife, Maria, was accomplished without firing a shot, even though they were all armed. The situation could have turned into a bloodbath as has been the case with the apprehension of several other extremist groups in this country. Fortunately, this arrest was conducted quickly and professionally by city policemen whose training and discipline prevented a shoot-out.

Raphael Anglada, one of our members at Reba Place, knew Maria Torres, her husband, Carlos, and one of the other persons who was arrested. Maria had been a high school senior in one of the classes that Raphael taught on the West Side of Chicago in 1972. About a year before the arrests, when the FBI was searching all over the country for FALN members, two agents talked to Raphael. Raphael had not heard from Carlos or Maria for several years, and so it was quite a shock when they turned up in Evanston. Why they were here is not certain. There is some suspicion that they were preparing to bomb the homes of three Democratic Convention delegates who support Jimmy Carter or possibly the home of U.S. Representative John Porter.

As crude as it may seem according to the ideals of nonviolence, tear gas is better than clubs, clubs are better than guns, and even guns can be used in a variety of ways. We should appreciate any evidence of restraint.

4. *Don't forget grace.* Violence is a product of sin. God desires peace and abhors violence. If our hearts are in tune with God's heart, we can trust that He will understand and be forgiving at the points where we fail. This certainly does not justify violence; it simply recognizes our frailty. Without grace we can become immobilized with the fear that we will do something wrong and thereby not live up to God's ideal.

It is important that we pass on this understanding and extend our personal forgiveness to our children when they lash out, especially if they have attempted to be peaceful and tolerant. If we don't extend forgiveness, our children will be crippled by guilt or reject as impossible and irrelevant the teachings about peace.

In fact, if we fail to extend grace to others, we will eliminate it (at least within our own minds) for ourselves.

5. *Love not the world.* God made humans gregarious, to need and enjoy one another's company. But our modern cities don't necessarily fulfill that need. In fact, anonymity is often a characteristic and an objective of urban living. The church, especially when it is formed into intentional community, can combat this problem.

Some people "groove" on the city and like being "where the action is." But in some cases what they have grown to love is not other people or wholesome relationships. It is the negative products of this world's system which excite them. They are indiscriminately titillated by the big creations of man—big buildings, big noise, big business, "big shots," and big crime. Even great poverty and pain excites their curiosity.

It is important that we do not enjoy what is evil. In fact, we should carefully resist a complacent attitude which is unoffended by overcrowding, pornography, drug abuse, noise, pollution, and crime. Tolerance for these things is not maturity but depravity.

6. *Yield to God's will.* When Joshua was commissioned as God's spokesman, Israel responded by saying to him, "All that you have commanded us we will do" (Joshua 1:16). Even though we declare Jesus to be our Lord, it is hard to live that way because it means we must frequently change. Our fears, our experiences, and even our theories must yield. Too often we begin with our theories and seek God's support, and this is true of those who would be nonviolent as well as those who justify violence. So it is important to ask ourselves again and again whether we are willing to change if the Lord so directs. Can we say with Jesus, "Not my will, but thine, be done"?

13
City of Refuge

The seven years of Barbara's marriage became a nightmare. She wondered whether she would be able to hold out until she could take care of her children on her own. Or would she be killed and mutilated suddenly if her outraged husband lost all control! Greg's explosions had become frequent and unpredictable. He was more and more obsessed with the martial arts, his black-belt degrees, and the destruction he could accomplish with his hands. His whole body was like steel, hardened and tuned by the constant rehearsal of his skills.

Even more frightening was the importance he placed on carrying out his threats of revenge. It was as though he felt he had to save face by fulfilling his angry words.

Barbara was terrified.

Greg's threats, which had sometimes focused on his employer or someone else with whom he had argued, now included Barbara. Sometimes he'd practice his martial arts on her just to show her how strong he was. She wasn't sure how often it was a macabre source of humor to him and when he was barely restraining his rage.

Finally, the day came when, with the help of her sister

who also lived in Miami, Barbara thought she could make it on her own. She left the children at the police station and went with a couple of officers to the apartment to get her personal belongings. Greg was upset, but he didn't seem particularly angry when she told him what she was doing. The police said that it was their policy to stay no more than five minutes in a domestic case. Barbara was afraid that at any moment Greg would begin pummeling her with bone-shattering blows when the police left, but he didn't. Greg talked to her for a while and said that he didn't want her to take the car. But he said he'd drive her to the police station, which he did.

The next day as Barbara was getting settled at her sister's house, Greg called and insisted that they meet somewhere to talk. As Barbara discussed the matter with her sister's husband, he encouraged her to consider the alternatives and not go to the meeting automatically. "Not only is it dangerous," he said, "but if you agree to this meeting, he'll continue to lead you around by the nose. You have to put your foot down and make your stand."

When Barbara phoned Greg and told him that she had decided not to meet with him, he became very upset. In a trembling voice he said, "I'm going to get you!"

Barbara knew that when he spoke like that he meant what he said, and it was serious. So she packed her things back up and took off with her children to her other sister's home in Minneapolis, nearly 1,800 miles away. Nearly nine months of peace followed for Barbara. She rented an apartment nearby and found a job to support herself and her children. She was corresponding with an attorney back in Miami who had once tried to get her a divorce.

Over several months he forwarded some unopened letters he'd been given by Greg. In those letters Greg vowed that he would find her and dismember and mutilate her. Barbara was terrified.

A few days later when she phoned her sister to ask if she could come over and borrow something, her sister said in a subdued voice, "No. Don't come now. Greg's here."

"Greg's there?"

"Yes. Somehow he got our address from the attorney in Miami and flew up here."

"Well, what's he want?" asked Barbara.

"He wants you, and he's threatening us if we don't give him your address. You've got to get out of town."

Barbara gathered the kids and went to Madison, Wisconsin, to stay with some friends that her sister had recommended. They were Christians and placed Barbara in the home of another family from their church for temporary shelter. Barbara's sister had requested that she locate herself in a "blind" place so that if Greg pressured her further she wouldn't know where to direct him.

Greg returned to Barbara's sister's home in Minneapolis several times. Finally they secured a peace bond against him, and when he returned to threaten them again, they called the police and he was thrown in jail for two weeks.

Barbara knew that she couldn't return to live in Minneapolis with Greg so close to finding her, so she began trying to find someplace else to move. She remembered having heard about Reba Place, so she contacted the Fellowship and made the arrangements.

While Greg was in jail in Minneapolis, she returned to her apartment and packed up her belongings and moved to Reba Place Fellowship in Evanston, Illinois. In describing what it was like for her, a non-Christian, to come to the Fellowship, she said, "When I arrived I first came to Maranatha Household. I thought the building looked kind of ugly, actually. Then Dennis Chesley, one of the elders, came out and took us down to the basement where his office was. There was play equipment there in the other part of the basement, and my kids started playing. I started crying because I had this sense of well-being that we would be free of all the fear that we'd been living with for so long.

"Also, when I went to worship for the first time, I brought a dollar because I didn't know that the Fellowship didn't take a collection. But the service was so moving to me in reassuring me of my safety in God that I ended up using that dollar as a handkerchief, I was crying so much. I had a real sense of peace that this was a haven for me."

Later, Barbara became a Christian and joined the Fellowship. She's been here for four years without any further harassment from Greg, but even if he did show up, Barbara says that she feels there is enough security here that she could stay and face him in the strength of the Lord.

o   o   o

A somewhat similar situation has not worked out so well.

When Patty Lou fled to Madison to the Shelter for Women she was assigned to Phyllis, a social worker who had been familiar with Barbara's case and successful relocation at Reba Place. As Phyllis heard Patty Lou's story, she began to think of Reba as an out-of-state refuge where she could send Patty Lou and the kids for safety from her husband, Jeff's, violent abuse.

Patty Lou had tried to leave Jeff on numerous occasions only to have him track her down, beat her up, and take her home. This time Patty Lou was seeking professional help. Jeff's abuse had escalated beyond violence to her and her boys, ages four, five, and six (all by a previous marriage). He had taken to throwing their one-year-old daughter (for

whom he was the father) against the wall or crib and knock-
ing her out when he was irritated by her crying. Patty Lou
knew she had to escape permanently.

After a good deal of negotiation with the Madison Shelter
for Women, Reba Place agreed to receive Patty Lou and the
children. We knew we were making ourselves vulnerable to
a violent and determined man, but it seemed a loving thing
to do, and Patty Lou came from a Baptist background and
was interested in relating to a church. The transfer was made
with several precautions. Following the recommendations of
the social worker, Patty Lou and the children took on
assumed names so that their identity would not accidentally
be revealed if Jeff got wind of the fact that they had moved
to the Chicago area and came looking for them. For many
months, no one in the Fellowship knew Patty Lou's or the
children's real names.

Martha Faw, one of our household managers, accepted
the responsibility of coordinating things for Patty Lou and
the children. Martha helped them find an apartment, enroll
the kids in school, and cut through the red tape of the
various social agencies necessary for their support. And finally, Martha got them all into family therapy through a
local hospital.

Phyllis, the social worker from the Madison Shelter for
Women, continued to complete the paperwork necessary to
obtain a legal separation or divorce which would enjoin Jeff
from seeing or harassing Patty Lou or the children. Martha
saw several of the police and doctor's reports that Phyllis ob-
tained, and they substantiated many of the stories Patty Lou
told about Jeff's violence. There was Patty Lou's sister who
had been beaten and raped. There was the neighbor who
had been hit over the head with a two by four when he tried
to intervene in Jeff's abuse of the family. There were the

many occasions the children were treated for injuries by the doctor in the small town outside of Madison where they lived. There was the police officer whom Jeff had beaten up. In all these incidents, any charges that had been filed were later mysteriously dropped.

From the beginning, in agreeing to invite Patty Lou, we had decided that we would not hesitate to call the police if Jeff showed up and tried forcefully to take Patty Lou with him. It was not a decision with which everyone was completely comfortable. But with our limited resources, it was the only condition under which we would accept the family. They would not be living in our households. Patty Lou was not prepared to assume the risk of our convictions, and there were the stories of Jeff's wild violence. Even though he wasn't a large man, he was said to have once disabled or overpowered seven other men who tried to restrain him.

Things went well for about two months. Then Patty Lou began writing to her sister who still lived in their hometown. She knew that Jeff frequently went over to her sister's house, so she did not put her return address on the outside of the envelope. But her sister was tired of sending letters back to Patty Lou through the social worker in Madison, so Patty Lou included her Evanston address inside a letter. Apparently Jeff found it or intercepted it.

One Saturday night not long after that, Jeff showed up at Patty Lou's apartment. He pleaded with her to come back to live with him, promising that things would be different, that he was sorry for the way he had treated her, and that he'd cut off his hands before he'd ever hurt the children again. Then he began saying that if she didn't come back, he couldn't go on living. Then his threats shifted to what he'd do to her to make her come back. Finally he began insisting that she give him Joanna, their baby girl. When Patty Lou refused, Jeff shoved her aside, took the baby, and ran.

A woman in the next apartment had heard some of the arguing and surmised that there was trouble. She was part of the Fellowship and had learned to know Patty Lou pretty well. She called the police, Martha Faw, and a couple of Fellowship elders.

Jeff no sooner ran around the corner and jumped into his dark green pickup with the baby than the police wheeled up and blocked his way with a squad car. In a moment a couple other cars arrived. They took everyone down to the police station to determine what had happened or should happen to resolve the problem.

Strangely enough, Patty Lou's sister had been waiting in the pickup. Jeff had talked her into coming down with him, convincing her that all he wanted was to get the family back together. The extent to which she had cooperated in giving away Patty Lou's location was never determined. On the other hand, Patty Lou's foolish decision to send her address, knowing Jeff's persistence and involvement with her sister, is hard to understand.

The police returned Joanna to her mother and warned Jeff to stay completely away from the area. They brought him and Patty Lou's sister back to his pickup and escorted them out of town.

In spite of the trauma of the event, Patty Lou decided that she wasn't going to run. It seemed to her that even though Jeff now knew her location, she was safer there than if she would go elsewhere. Everyone in the Fellowship was alerted to the possibility of Jeff's return. The police were more watchful of the neighborhood and prepared to respond quickly. Patty Lou intensified her efforts to obtain a divorce which would establish custody of the children and enjoin Jeff to stay away except by special arrangement. While the divorce was pending, a local judge did issue a temporary restraining order forbidding Jeff to harass the family or remove any of the children from the premises of the mother's dwelling.

Since Jeff was aware of their location, Patty Lou and the children dropped their assumed names. In some ways things were less tense. She had made her decision; she was taking a stand, and it was out in the open. She had a broad support network around her, and on the recommendation of her social worker she was pursuing all the legal channels available to her for protection—divorce, custody, court order, and a responsive and gracious police department.

Jeff did come back once in the next few days, and Patty Lou called the police immediately. They quickly chased him out of town but did not catch him.

And then, five weeks after Jeff's first visit, a woman came to Patty Lou's door at about eight in the morning and said, "I'm here to babysit for the children."

Patty Lou needed babysitting that morning because she had a family therapy appointment at the hospital. She had made arrangements with another mother, but that had fallen through and the mother had said, "Since I can't do it, I'll see if I can find someone else for you."

The sitter was more than an hour early, and Patty Lou didn't know the slovenly dressed woman who had come to her door. But probably she was connected to the Fellowship, Patty Lou thought. How could anyone else know that she needed babysitting on a Friday morning? Patty Lou was still new enough to the Fellowship that she didn't know everybody, and besides, the woman could have been an approved guest sent over by the hospitality committee.

Patty Lou invited her in, and the woman began trying to get acquainted with the children. The older two boys had

gone to school, so it was just the youngest boy and the tod-
dler, Joanna, who were there. When it neared the time for
Patty Lou to leave for the hospital, the woman suggested
that she take the children out for an ice-cream cone as a
good way to gain their confidence. That seemed good to
Patty Lou, and she said good-bye.

The woman walked the children down the street about a
block and a half to where Jeff was waiting with another man
in a car. They put Joanna in the car, but Jeff said to the little
boy, "I don't want you. Get out of here. Go home to your
mother." And they raced off.

A Fellowship member found the boy wandering back
down the street crying. He said, "My daddy came and took
away my sister." We called the police and Patty Lou at the
hospital and sent someone to pick her up. By the time the
boy was able to give any kind of a description of the car, Jeff
and the others were beyond interception.

Immediately the Evanston Police contacted the sheriff
having jurisdiction over the small town where Jeff lived.
However, the sheriff would not respond. He did not return
the calls or cooperate in any way. The FBI was contacted,
but because the father of the child was involved, they were
not sure a formal charge of kidnapping across state lines
would hold, so they declined to get involved.

Joanna's safety was complicated not only by Jeff's violent
history, but by the fact that the hospital staff had diagnosed
Joanna as a severely disturbed child prone to seizure-like
episodes resulting from the previous trauma in her life. Jeff
did not know about the fact that she would sometimes vomit
and stop breathing. And he knew nothing of the medication
that had been prescribed for her.

The whole community entered into prayer for the safe
return of the baby and for the peace of the boys and Patty

Lou. The family was scheduled for dinner in different homes to break up the sense of waiting for the phone to ring. Martha Faw's phone was listed with the police and the other social agencies as a place Patty Lou could be reached if she weren't home.

Two weeks later Jeff phoned Patty Lou and threatened both her life and the life of the baby. Patty Lou could hear Joanna crying in the background, so she knew she was still alive, but the call was terrifying. That call escalated the seriousness of Jeff's technical offenses from having violated the court's restraining order to the use of the telephone to threaten murder. An additional warrant was issued with these charges, and the police put a tap on Patty Lou's phone not only to tape any further threats, but hopefully to trace Jeff's location.

Even under these more serious conditions the sheriff in Wisconsin was reluctant to help. Patty Lou began to get word from people in her hometown that they saw Jeff from time to time. Once someone told the sheriff that they had just seen Jeff, but the sheriff was so slow in responding that Jeff was gone by the time the sheriff arrived.

The time dragged on. A few days later Jeff phoned again and made many violent threats. This time he said that if Patty Lou did not come back to him, he had no reason to live, and he would kill himself and the baby. The baby was crying so much in the background that there was concern that he may have been doing something to provoke the crying. Janalee Croegaert, another mother in the Fellowship, overheard this frightening conversation on an extension phone. However, when the police went to check their tap, it had been removed the day before Jeff's call.

Jeff had some relatives who worked for the telephone company. Whether or not he learned from them how to fake an order to remove a tap, we don't know. The phone company said it had been removed by accident. The police were indignant and replaced it with instructions that it was not to be removed again until they said to remove it. However, two days later when Jeff called again, the tap had just been removed. The police had it put back on, but it never did provide a clear lead to him. The calls were too short to trace, and then they began to decrease in frequency until they finally quit.

Three months later Patty Lou's divorce came through, and she was granted exclusive custody of the children. This provided an additional legal advantage for Patty Lou, but the time and tension were taking a toll on her endurance. In the meantime her first husband showed up. He had heard a rumor that one of the boys had died. After finding that all was well with them (they were his boys), he decided to stay in the neighborhood. Apart from our counsel, Patty Lou began seeing him regularly, even before the divorce came through. He wanted her and the boys to live with him.

Without the cooperation of the sheriff in Wisconsin, the Evanston Police could do little more. Patty Lou enlisted the efforts of the Wisconsin State's Attorney, and the Madison Shelter for Women was able to get the media to put some pressure on the situation. Then the next month, in January, some hope seemed to dawn. An election replaced the sheriff with a new one. He promised to be more cooperative.

Finally the welfare people went with one of the sheriff's men to Jeff's house and took pictures of the baby through the window. Jeff came out with a shotgun and chased them away. After that the sheriff said that he wasn't going to have anything more to do with the case. "The life of one of my men was threatened when they went out there to take those pictures. He hasn't committed a crime in my county, and as far as I am concerned, no problem exists. If somebody else has a warrant for him, they can go get him.''

The women's shelter and the welfare department then enlisted a lawyer to prepare papers which, when approved by a judge, would be served through the state's attorney to the sheriff giving him temporary custody of the baby and forcing him to go and get the baby.

For this complicated and risky maneuver it was necessary for Patty Lou to go back to Wisconsin and be there for the event. When the time came, she left her boys with Martha Faw and made the trip. She chose to have her first husband drive her there.

Unfortunately, the lawyer had been too busy to draw up the papers. So the action had not been approved by a judge, and nothing could be done. Patty Lou was crushed. To her it seemed like the last straw in a nightmare that had been going on for about seven months since Jeff had first tried to abduct the child.

She was tired of it all and felt guilty for being too tired to keep fighting for her baby. It felt impossible. It was too much to cope with. Escape would be a relief, and her first husband kept offering that to her.

She returned to Evanston and, the next day, without making any arrangements with the boys' school, the family therapist, Martha Faw, or anyone else from the Fellowship who had been helping her, she took the boys and left.

We've since learned from some of her relatives where she and her first husband have relocated. Patty Lou doesn't seem to be making any further effort to retrieve Joanna. We still pray for everyone involved. Maybe we did all we could do. Maybe the amount that the police were involved was necessary—the best possible course, given the circumstances. We're still learning.

14
Broken Chains

John Thomson reread the letter from his sister as he sat on the edge of his bunk. She had heard from his father, whom the family hadn't seen for eight years. John had been only nine at the time his parents separated. Before that he mostly remembered how his dad used to come home raving drunk and beat the family. Once John was nearly thrown out of the apartment window by his father.

But the letter said that his father had cirrhosis of the liver, and, before he died, he wanted to visit John in the reformatory. John felt good about that even though he and his dad had never been very close. John wished that he could get out of the "hole" before his dad came. Waiting in his cell without being allowed to work or participate in any recreation and being completely segregated from any of the other boys was hard. The time went so slowly. He wished that he could talk to somebody. Possibly, if he behaved himself, he would be let out of the hole before his dad came.

Then one day the captain, a sergeant, and a case worker called John into an office. As John walked in and sat down, he hoped they were going to tell him about a date for the visit.

"John, tell us about your father," one of them said.

"What do you want to know?"

"Well, what kind of a man was he?"

John began to be a little apprehensive. Somewhere in the back of his mind he had the impression that his dad had been in prison. As a child he remembered sitting in a courtroom once; he thought that had been a domestic fight, but maybe it had been more. If his father did have a record, the authorities at the Illinois Industrial School for Boys in Sheridan might not allow his father to see him. John answered: "Well, I don't know. Okay, I guess. What do you mean?"

"When was the last time you saw him?"

"Eight years ago when my folks separated."

"Did he ever take you on any picnics?"

"No. I can't remember any."

"Well, did he ever take you to a ball game?"

"Yeah. He took me to one."

"Just one?"

"I only remember one. But so what? I was so small that I can't remember much about it."

"Then you and your dad didn't have a very close relationship, did you?"

"No. I was mostly afraid of him."

"Well, good," said the captain. "Since it's been so long since you have seen your father and since he never did anything for you, he obviously didn't love you. So we don't think that you should feel too bad about his being dead."

John sat in silence for a few moments. "Can I go to the funeral?"

"No. That's what we were saying. We don't think you should feel too bad. Now go back to your cell."

That night John allowed himself to cry, but they were

tears of bitterness and anger, not grief. His life had never been an easy one. Maybe the captain was right, and his dad didn't love him. His mom had often told him that if he kept getting in trouble, he'd be in prison before he was 21. After his parents had separated, he'd started running away from home, turning in false fire alarms, and shoplifting so often that at the age of nine his mother sent him away to a military school for boys in Glenwood, Illinois. While he was in the school his mother remarried and moved from Chicago to Hazelcrest, a nearby community. But she seldom visited him, and he didn't know how close she lived to him until he got out of the school at the age of 13. At that time he tried to return to his family, but he couldn't get along with his new stepfather.

Along with the poor home situation, John remembers that he had difficulty adjusting to a nonstructured life. In some ways he had done well in the institutional environment of the military school and "civilian" life seemed abnormal to him. He couldn't get along with kids in public school, and drifted into more and more trouble until he stole a car at the age of 14.

The court put him on probation and had him live with a long-standing friend of the family, "Aunt" Dorothy. She had been one of the most positive influences on John, but he still didn't make a turnaround. In two months he stole another car. This began a sequence of juvenile homes, escapes, further crime, two more auto thefts, and finally reformatory at St. Charles, Illinois.

There he stayed for 17 months which was much longer than the usual first-time stay of six to nine months. Unless a clerical error omitted his name from consideration for parole, John figures that he was detained because his family would not agree to accept him back. At St. Charles, John was introduced to far more serious crime since the institution housed murderers, rapists, and armed robbers as well as the deliquents and incorrigible troublemakers. He soon learned the rudiments of surviving in a violent institution.

At 16 John was released to return to his home, but within six months his stepfather kicked him out of the house. When the parole officer discovered this, John was returned to a youth work camp. He felt that was unfair since he hadn't committed a crime but had just been kicked out of the house by a stepfather who cared little for him anyway. For this, John decided that he would escape, which he did a couple of times, then was sent to Sheridan Boys School. That was his first experience in a real prison with double barbed wire, guard towers, and the "hole"—the isolation cells where uncooperative prisoners were confined as punishment.

John was sent to Sheridan because he kept running away and declared that he would continue trying to run away because he considered himself unjustly confined. But most of the prisoners were there because of their violence—either violent crimes or violent behavior in lower security institutions. Survival was for the fittest, and that meant either the meanest or the craziest. And in an institution which was 80 percent black, John, a white, had to overcompensate. Out of his 26 months at Sheridan, he spent 16 of them in the hole.

That night in the hole after hearing of his father's death, John vowed never again to allow anybody to hurt him and that he would do his best to pay the world back for the raw deal he felt he had gotten from life. He promised himself that no matter what happened, no matter how rough things got, he'd never shed another tear.

This was the excuse John gave himself for any wrong he did from then on. It also became his strength. In fact, in the future if he didn't feel mad enough about a situation to have the courage to pull some crime, he would deliberately think back to the time in Sheridan and dwell on the way the captain told him about his father's death. That was always sufficient to make him angry enough so that he didn't care what happened to himself. For the next ten years he lived out that vow.

When he was 19 he was paroled. At first he tried to live with his older sister. When that didn't work, he returned to his mother's home. Two months after his release he and a friend stole another car and drove it across state lines. That made the crime a Federal offense, and he remembers feeling a sense of status in the courtroom at the idea that it was the whole United States of America vs. John Thomson.

He was sentenced to the Federal Correctional Institution for youth in Ashland, Kentucky. That was a less violent place than Sheridan, but John stayed there only 13 months. A riot occurred, and though he wasn't an instigator, he did participate along with 350 other inmates. Afterwards, however, because of being one of the older ones, the administration said that he was one of 20 leaders in the riot. He was sent to the Federal Reformatory in El Reno, Oklahoma.

El Reno was mean; it was known as "Gladiator's School." One never knew when someone would jump out of a garbage can and stab you for no reason at all. An inmate had to be on his guard every moment he wasn't in a cell by himself.

In all the institutions, the administration frequently cajoled the inmates by saying, "You better shape up or you're going to be sent up to . . . [the next 'higher' institution], and you'll never make it there." The threat was a challenge for most who heard it. The inmates wanted to prove that they were tough enough to "make it."

John quickly made his way in El Reno. Within a week he

was marked as a troublemaker—responsible for trying to start another riot.

Finally, he was sent to the Federal Penitentiary in Marion, Illinois. El Reno had been a reformatory; Marion was a Federal penitentiary, rated the most secure prison in the country. John realized he had fulfilled the predictions his mother had made when he was seven and eight years old: he was in a real penitentiary before his twenty-first birthday.

Most of the prisoners who had been in the maximum-security federal penitentiary on Alcatraz Island when it closed down had been transferred to Marion. Many were in for life. John learned what Marion was all about in his first week. Two guys were playing cards. One laid his knife on the table and the other placed a length of metal pipe on the table. Halfway through the game the guy with the knife decided he wasn't going to pay. He grabbed his knife and stabbed his opponent in the left hand. But with his right hand, the other inmate grabbed his pipe and killed the first one with one blow over the head.

In that stint John served a little over three and a half years of a six-year sentence before he was paroled. But the whole effect of Marion on John was a challenge to be tougher and meaner than the next guy. Like a caged cat, he was ready to pounce when he was released on July 6, 1967. By the 11th he had already burglarized an insurance company. But it was 55 days after his release before he was arrested again. During that time he commited four burglaries, two armed robberies, a house break-in, and a kidnapping. None of this was because John lacked money. He had a job during this time and cleared $200 a week working at an asphalt company.

Most of the crimes were done because they were possible. He burglarized the insurance office because an employee, who happened to be John's friend, foolishly revealed where a key was hidden which opened the door. John was insensitive to the loyalties and honor that should accompany friendship. Crime was his life, and he was living it out.

One night John and another ex-convict were driving around. They had a .45 pistol and were looking for a job to pull. They stopped at a gas station, and after they filled the car with gas, John said to the attendant, "Get me a pack of cigarettes, okay?"

"Get them yourself," the attendant said. So John got the cigarettes himself. As they left the station, the rebuff began eating at John's pride. He turned to his partner and said, "Let's go back and hit that guy."

So they went back to the station and robbed the attendant. Then they realized that the station was right across the street from a police station. If they just drove off, the police would be after them too quickly, so they tied the attendant up, put him in the backseat, and started to drive out to the forest preserve.

The power of the gun was intoxicating, and John began talking to his buddy about going coast to coast. With a gun he felt he could do just about anything he wanted to do. He wondered what it would be like to kill somebody. For a long time while in prison he had been prepared to kill in self-defense. He knew he was ready for that. But he was uncertain whether he had the nerve to face the prison sentence for killing someone in cold blood. Could he do it? It became an obsession to John, and he fell into a near trance.

When they arrived at the forest preserve, they told the attendant to get out and start walking without looking back. John leaned out the door and drew a bead on the back of the man's head dimly lit by the reflected lights of the city. He was steady. He knew he could do it. He was pulling the hammer back when his buddy yelled, "Don't shoot him!"

John snapped out of the trance, and they drove away.

When John was finally arrested at the end of his 55 days of freedom, he was sent to Cook County Jail to await his trial. He found Cook to be one of the worst of the series of prisons which were yet to follow.

When the trial was finally completed several months later, John received nothing more than a sentence of two to four years for all the offenses during his spree. That was the result of plea bargaining in a court that is so busy that it couldn't afford the delays a sharp lawyer could throw into the case. John served his time for these crimes in Stateville Penitentiary in Joliet, Illinois, and the state penitentiary in Menard, Illinois.

When he was released in August of 1970, John avoided any involvement in crime for several weeks. But in December he was arrested for unlawful use of a weapon, after pulling several burglaries, and spent five months in the state penitentiary in Vandalia, Illinois.

During the two months after his release from Vandalia John avoided arrest for several burglaries, but he began to feel more and more depressed about the way trouble followed him around. Once he went to Wisconsin to get away from his problems and took a low-paying job in a hotel. However, the second night after he started work, in walked his youngest brother and an older ex-con. They were on the run from the police after an attempted burglarly and didn't have any money.

John felt this was proof that trouble followed him everywhere he went, so he lifted $800 from the till and took off with his brother and partner for St. Louis. On the way they robbed a liquor store. Finally, John decided that he needed to send his brother, who was only 16, back home.

John and his partner started casing a savings and loan bank. Finally, even though he felt nervous about the set up, John said, "We've waited long enough. Either we're going to hit this bank or not, but let's get on with it."

They had an automatic pistol and a rifle, but the idea of carrying the rifle inside of a flower box didn't make sense, so John bought a toy cap pistol which looked realistic and agreed to use it.

At a time when there were only four employees on duty, John and his partner ran into the bank. John jumped over the counter to make sure the alarm was not sounded. They corralled the people and tied their hands behind their backs. Then John's partner cleaned all of the money out of the drawers. John started to leave, mindful that staying in a bank more than two minutes was said to be foolish.

"No. Let's get the vault first," said his partner as he went in, careful not to set off the alarm. When he came out, they had about $10,000 altogether.

"We got to get out of here," said John.

"What are we going to do with these people?"

"Just leave them. Let's go."

"They'll get the cops the moment we go out the door."

"Well then, put them in the vault."

"Okay." And they herded the people into the vault and started to close the door.

"Wait a minute. Aren't these things air tight?"

"So what?"

"They might suffocate, and I don't want that on me."

"Yeah. Okay, get them out of there. I'll see what's behind that door."

It was a stairway to a basement room, but when they had put the people into the vault, they had unknowingly tripped the alarm. And by the time the people were secured in the basement, the police had started to surround the place. They ran into an adjoining office with a door out of the back, but it was locked. John jumped into a closet thinking that the police wouldn't know how many robbers were involved and hoping that by the time the people in the basement told, the police would assume that he had escaped.

They arrested his partner, and then they came looking for John. During the time that the search went on, John just gave up. He knew that he would be found, go to jail, go through the courts, and back to prison for 15 years at the least, even if he pled guilty. When he heard the police at the door, he moved to a place where he could be seen when they opened the door but a place where he hoped that he wouldn't surprise them too much.

The door opened and the young cop jumped, so startled that he almost pulled the trigger. He stood there shaking with his gun pointed at John's head yelling, "You want to die? You want to die? Just move and you can die."

At first John and his partner decided to plead guilty, hoping to receive the lightest possible sentence. (They discovered that in Missouri it would not be 15 but 18 years.) Then, as John sat in jail waiting for his trial, he began to think about his life.

He was 27 years old. Except for the various periods of a few months duration when he was out and committing crimes, he had been in institutions for the last 18 years—11 of them in jails, reformatories, or prisons. To him institutional life was normal and freedom was abnormal. He had never learned to live successfully on his own. The outside world was alien, and he was not equipped to meet it. As John thought about it, he felt it was like taking a lion which had been raised in captivity and placing it out in the wild and expecting it to survive. If it lived at all, it would probably do so by raiding villages and farms.

He wrapped his whole life up in an accusation of the system. It wasn't fair for prison to be normal but horrible, and outside to be nice but so abnormal to him that he couldn't survive in it.

So John decided to withdraw his guilty plea and entered a plea of not guilty by reason of insanity. He knew that the issue of sanity in legal terms had nothing to do with his line of reasoning. All that a court was interested in was determining whether a person knew what he was doing at the time of committing the crime and whether he was able to understand the proceedings and help in his own defense in the courtroom. By these criteria, John knew that he was as sane as the judge, and his public defender thought his efforts were completely foolish and would only get him a longer sentence in the end. But he stuck with his plan, and was finally sent to the Medical Center for Federal Prisoners at Springfield, Missouri, for observation.

At this point it may be best to let John tell about the next stage of his life as he has written it down.

o   o   o

One Sunday morning in May 1972, nearly a year after the bank robbery, a young prisoner came into my room at the Springfield Medical Center telling about one of the funniest things he'd ever seen when he'd gone to church that morning. What he had seen was prisoners testifying to having accepted Jesus as their Savior and saying such things as "Praise the Lord" and "Amen."

I didn't find it so amusing. People did a lot of strange things. Even the prison orientation booklet encouraged "doing your own time." If that was how these dudes wanted to do their time, then more power to them.

Ironically, though, the next Sunday as I left the chow hall, a group of visitors passed going to the church service. Hearing a bunch of guys say, "Praise the Lord," didn't interest me, but there were a few young ladies among the visitors. So, inasmuch as Sundays are about the most boring day of the week, and since a guy seldom gets to see women while in prison, I went for the first time in a decade.

Church and God were just not a part of my life in any way, shape, or form. I had almost no idea of what was meant by being a Christian. My strongest emotions were hate and anger against almost everyone and everything.

I continued going to church for a month, watching the girls and speaking to no one. Since there was a lot of preaching and testifying by other prisoners, I had to listen to what they had to say. It sounded nice but unrealistic for someone in prison. Hatred was almost as essential for survival in prison as was carrying a shank (a homemade knife), and who could love his brother among such a bunch of cutthroats? Two things developed inside me that caused me to speak out against the teachings. I knew that there were other men in the meetings who felt as deeply bitter against the world as I did, but no one was saying anything. I was not so passive. If I did not accept what was being said, I decided that I would question it, especially when these visitors were coming onto "my ground" to say it.

Also, I soon tired of these people coming into the prison to shine their halos on our tarnished lives. No one needed to tell me that I was a sinner. I lived with the results of my sin each waking hour. I never thought of myself as deceiving the world by trying to be something which I wasn't . . . which is how I judged most church people.

So I decided that I was going to speak my mind whether it was acceptable or not. The Bible instructor was confi-

dently expounding on the subject of everyone being born
with a free will and our supposed freedom to choose. I, just
as confidently, raised my hand and stated my case to the
contrary.

"One doesn't even have the choice to be born," I said.
"Nor does he choose who his parents will be. He can't
choose whether he will be loved or rejected, born in poverty
or riches. He doesn't choose if he will be reared on the Gold
Coast or in the ghetto, and when he comes up short on each
count and strikes back at the ill fate he had no choice in
receiving in the first place, he ends up in prison. And now
you tell me I've got a freedom to choose. Most prisoners at
some time in their development reject the same society
which has rejected them. They reject its values, morals, and
religion. You cannot train a man for freedom while he is in
captivity, and for many men, their captivity began the day
they were born."

That church became very quiet with all eyes on the Bible
instructor or me. The instructor stammered and stuttered a
response to the effect that he would answer me after the
meeting was over. But to his convenience he became involved in other conversations, which I took to mean he
didn't want to deal with the statement I had made.

However, as I prepared to leave, a little old lady in her sev-
enties quickly approached me and said, "Jesus loves you,
and even though you don't understand it, He has a plan and
purpose for your life." To be sure, I didn't understand it! I
left the church quickly and determined that I would never
set foot in it again.

I had been taking some classes to help pass the time, so
the next morning I began my routine by going to class. As I
gave the teacher my pass to be signed, she said, "It was good
to see you in church yesterday." Then I recognized that she

had been one of the young ladies who had been coming as a visitor to the church services. In her role as a teacher, the grapevine had it that her family was quite wealthy, and so I figured that she had had it real easy all her life, safe and secure. I figured that she didn't know anything about prisons and even less about those who were confined in them.

I told her, "Yeah. I've been going every week, but it's not done me much good." After which I spun on my heels and retreated to my desk.

That night as I sought escape through sleep, I found myself troubled that I might have offended her. The thought was even more troubling because, even if I had, so what? I had never regretted anything I'd ever done, so why was I worried about the feelings of some girl I didn't even know. Still, I remained bothered about it until I finally determined that the next day I would go down to the school and apologize. Then I would never go to the school again.

While it seemed that most guys had become accustomed to women working inside the prison and addressed them on a first name basis, I hadn't accepted that they should even be there. So, when I entered the school that following day, I approached the teacher and said, "Miss Lipscomb, most men here believe you are genuine in your Christian beliefs, but God has never done anything for me, and I have never done anything for Him, so we're even. Now, if I said anything yesterday to offend you, I didn't mean to."

Then she said, "Did you ever ask Him?"

"Ask Him what?" I said.

"Did you ever ask Him to do anything for you?"

"Sure, I asked Him to get me out of Boy's School when I was 13, but He never did."

Then she went on to tell me that if I would pray and ask

Him, He would change me. I answered that it was too late for that. My life was wasted, and I would probably die in prison. I didn't need Him to help me do that.

We closed the conversation at that point, and I left the room.

But that night, I was again troubled . . . and angry that I had gone to apologize to a girl and that she had taken the opportunity to get the better of me by making her point. So I plotted to get even with her by using as excuses every ill-fated event that had ever happened to me as proofs that God did not want to do anything for me, so I didn't need Him.

Armed with all the heavy drama that my life contained, I again approached her with the idea that I'd put her in her place. As I rattled off excuse after excuse, she responded with a different verse of Scripture supporting her contention that God could change me if only I would accept Jesus Christ as my Savior.

Finally she said, "The choice is yours" (we were back to that again) "either to accept Him or reject Him. If you accept Him, He will forgive you and change you and give you a brand-new life. If you reject Him, then that's your choice, and you'll have to live with the consequences."

As I sat considering a response, I sensed that I was alone. Turning, I discovered that she had evened the score by walking off as I had done to her.

Troubled, sleepless nights became the expected thing after I started discussing God with Miss Lipscomb. At that point in my life I was pretty disgusted with everything and everyone. So many years in prison had warped my mind away from logical, rational ways of reasoning. The most I could hope for was to survive the ordeals of a continuous life in prison. Family and friends had long since deserted me, and all that I had left was my hatred as strength. Only the fleeting fantasy that someday, somehow, life might change kept me from suicide.

Ever since that time in reform school when I had made the vow to never let anyone get to me again and to make trouble for the rest of my time, I had lived out that resentment for the way the officials broke the news of my father's death to me. Now as I reviewed my life in my mind, weighing it against what the young lady had said, one persistent question illumined my thoughts. What if what that girl said was true? What if God could change me? The possibility was hard to grasp. Could I ever be anything but a convict in prison?

During my time in prison, many new progressive programs had been introduced to rehabilitate criminals, but I hadn't responded to any of them. If God was real, didn't I owe it to myself to let Him at least try to change me? Would I be any worse off if He couldn't?

For hours I wrestled with the possible consequences of attempting to become a Christian. The other convicts would reject me, but rejection wasn't anything new to me. And besides, hadn't I always done whatever I pleased regardless of what others thought? Hesitantly I began what I thought to be the most honest prayer that I could come up with: "Lord, I don't have much faith and very little hope, but if what that girl says is true and You can change me, then I accept You as my Savior."

The next day as I hurried to school to tell Mary (I had decided that she wasn't too bad after all, and besides, I could use a friend), I sensed that I really didn't feel that much different. Later Mary told me that we are not to trust our feelings, but that the Christian life is lived by faith.

The following Sunday I sat in the church service with Mary and a newfound sense of expectancy. As I listened to the guest speaker and singer (Larry Norman) that day, the sense of expectancy changed to a confidence in the presence of the Lord, and I knew as sure as anything can be known that the Lord was real in my life.

"It was good to see you in church yesterday." It is kind of hard to believe that the Lord could use that one little sentence to begin to change my whole world around.

o   o   o

Six years later John turned in his fifth petition for parole. Each previous time the board had rejected his request, saying, "Due to your past criminal history, there is no reasonable probability that you would be able to live at liberty without violating the law." During those six years, much had happened. John returned from Springfield after his period of observation competent to stand trial, but the judge was willing to listen to testimony concerning his Christian conversion and was willing to place John under 25 years of supervision by the U.S. Attorney General. If that plan had worked, John would have spent his nights in prison, but he could have worked at a local airport for a Christian man during the days.

However, the State of Wisconsin had filed a retainer against him for crimes he had committed there, and that prevented him from participating in a work release program. John was sent to the U.S. Penitentiary in Terre Haute, Indiana. There he did good time and remained involved with other Christians in prison. Not everything went smoothly, but his faith did grow.

Mary Lipscomb left Missouri and moved to Evanston to join Reba Place Fellowship, but she never forgot John or many of the other prisoners with whom she worked. Mary enlisted our prayers, assistance, and letters on behalf of John.

Other Christians with whom John had been corresponding also wrote to the parole board.

Finally, after his fifth request and without explanation, they reversed their previous decisions and released John. He came to Evanston to live near Reba Place. It has been hard to learn how to be free, hold a job, and cope with frustration and anger, but John is managing. By God's grace he has done more than simply live at liberty without violating the law. He has become fully involved in Chuck Colson's Prison Fellowship and has led our congregation and many other Christians in the beginnings of a ministry to prisoners.

After his first year of freedom, a group of Christian brothers and sisters in our church made John a white tunic, beautifully embroidered around the neck with flowers and a broken chain. John's chains which would have bound him for life and eternity have truly been broken.

At this time John has been free for two years. He is still serving the Lord. And he and Mary Lipscomb have announced their engagement to be married.

About that schoolteacher whom he thought didn't know very much, John says, "Well, we often ask each other: 'Now who would have ever imagined . . . ?' and the answer is 'The Lord!' "

15
Reflections IV: Scriptures

Many biblical passages could be studied in trying to discern how we should respond to crime and violence and whether we should call the police. However, I will restrict myself in this chapter to four points about how we as citizens of the kingdom of God are to conduct ourselves in this world. To begin with, we need to recognize clearly the distinction between the kingdom of God and the fallen, human social order which now prevails throughout the world—including the governments of our cities.

1. *Our civil institutions are not expressions of God's kingdom.* In Romans 13 and 1 Peter 2 we read that human governments have been instituted by God. Throughout the history of the church, these passages have been interpreted in various ways.

On one extreme are those who have assumed that whatever power exists in any given time or place must be God's will. They would say that if one's city government is corrupt, that's unfortunate, but it is nonetheless the government God has ordained. But how far should that thinking extend? What if the government is infiltrated by the Mafia? Or what if the neighborhood is controlled by a gang? A gang also constitutes a kind of government, not altogether distinguishable from some of the governments during biblical times, which of course were not elected by the will of the people but took their power by force. Wherever there is a vacuum of power, someone will always take control and create an order. It may be a fragmented order or an unjust order, but there will always be someone in power. Are we to assume, as did some theologians watching the rise of Hitler, that whatever order exists has been instituted by God?

On the other extreme, some have interpreted those Scriptures by noting that in the context, the purpose of government is stated as "punishing those who do wrong and praising those who do right." They would say that whenever a government fulfills this role it is legitimate and thereby ordained by God, but when it does not comply with God's design, it is illegitimate and should be replaced, by whatever means is necessary.

But both of these approaches expect the impossible from our civil institutions. They presume that our governments are or should be the expression of God's kingdom. And that is the mistake! The complete biblical record portrays earthly governments in more modest terms. It accepts them as necessary for the organization of human experience and it judges them accountable to the Lord, but the Bible also asserts that our human institutions are products of our fallen society, susceptible to man's every perversion, and potential vehicles for the efforts of the evil principalities and powers. This fact is graphically portrayed as "the beast" in Revelation 13.

When we are clear that the identity, origin, and purpose of the worldly governments are distinct from our primary identity, citizenship, and purpose as Christians, then we can better evaluate how we should relate to those institutions.

Even in the passage where Peter tells us to be subject to human institutions, he does so only after reminding us that we are *aliens* in this world's system (1 Peter 2:11). And Jesus made the same distinction at His trial by saying, "My kingship is not of this world; if my kingship were of this world, my servants would fight" (John 18:36). But His servants maintained their distinction; they did not fight, not even for the most just cause ever to offer itself in human history—the defense of the totally innocent Jesus of Nazareth.

The need for this distinction is sometimes forgotten when the cause of the worldly institution appears particularly worthy. And it is even harder to be clear if it appears that *God's hand* has worked through a civil authority, using a means (say, a violence which would be inconsistent with our kingdom identity) to accomplish some good end, such as the restoration of order or the prevention of some crime. Does the apparent good end justify our participation in the means? Not necessarily. God has a way of redeeming evil for good which should not lead us to justify that evil. For instance, in the Old Testament Joseph was sold into slavery by the evil deeds of his brothers. Later when he saved those brothers from famine, Joseph told them, "As for you, you meant evil against me; but God meant it for good" (Genesis 50:20). Or, much later in history, God is said to have used the Assyrians to punish the Hebrews for their sin. But did that justify Assyria's violent campaign? No. In Isaiah 10 God declared doom on the strident world conquerors, the very people He had allowed to serve His purpose.

We can admit that some things which are inconsistent with the kingdom still result in relative good. We may even consider some force necessary without enduing our civil institutions with the lofty role of being an arm of God's kingdom. God may use them in spite of their fallen nature, but He has never suggested that their character is righteous.

2. *Worldly governments should serve the kingdom.* Because of people's rebellion against the direct reign of God, God allowed the development of substitute governments so that mankind would not destroy itself by utter chaos. The substitute is not necessarily God's regent, carrying out and communicating His will, but His plan for redemption needed an environment of relative order in which to plant the kingdom.

This is why in Romans 13, Paul tells the believers that they must not participate in any insurrection, which they might have been inclined to do. The believers were not called to *obey* the government, which would have implied that the government was the mediator of God's will, but to *be subject* to it. This simply means not to rebel or act as though the government does not exist. Whether the Christians were to obey the authorities, or submit by accepting the punishment for their disobedience, depended upon what they were commanded to do.

It is the Christian's job to declare that Jesus is Lord over the human institutions and to call them and all of the principalities and powers behind them to bow before Him (Philippians 2:9, 10). Again, at His trial Jesus reminded Pilate, "You would have no power over me unless it had been given you from above" (John 19:11).

It is appropriate to call earthly governments to serve Christ and His kingdom, to prepare the way of the Lord by pursuing justice, caring for the poor, maintaining order, respecting the sanctity of life, supporting marriage and family, extending liberty, and outlawing evil. And with this challenge, we can communicate the promise of God's blessing. In Proverbs 31:9 we read, "Open your mouth, judge righteously, maintain the rights of the poor and needy."

This responsibility to speak out and call our governments to righteousness is not a call for them to be the kingdom but to serve the kingdom, and it is all the more our task to issue that call in a democracy where the government is said to function by the consent of the majority.

3. *Be subject to the government but not out of bondage.* Why do we honor our civil institutions? Many Christians do not know the reason. But the Bible tells us why we are to give such honor in the very passages where it instructs us to do so, and the reason is very important lest we confuse, as many Christians have, the command with a mandate for universal obedience.

In 1 Peter 2 the reasons are clear: "Maintain good conduct among the Gentiles, *so that in case they speak against you as wrongdoers, they may see your good deeds* and glorify God on the day of visitation" (v. 12, emphasis added). The fact that the believers could expect to be spoken against as wrongdoers shows that they did not always conform. But in the searing light of judgment day, even the pagans will acknowledge that the deeds of the believers were actually good and praise God for their faithfulness. The passage goes on, "Be subject *for the Lord's sake* to every human institution. . . . For it is God's will that *by doing right you should put to silence the ignorance of foolish men*" (vv. 13, 15, emphasis added).

All of this advice is given in the qualifying context of verse 11 in which Peter reminds the believers that they are aliens in their setting. Their true allegiance is to God alone whom they serve and fear, rather than the emperor from whom they were to consider themselves free. They were to honor the emperor as they honored all people (vv. 16, 17).

We do not obey the government because we fear it or are in bondage to it. We do not obey it because it is the highest authority. We do not obey it because it mediates God's will to us. We can be glad whenever it requires people to do what is right, but if it presses us to participate in evil, we must declare with Peter and the apostles (as well as Daniel and the saints of the Old Testament) that "we must obey God rather than men" (Acts 5:29). For that stand we may suffer persecution, but as Peter says, "If one suffers as a Christian, let him not be ashamed, but under that name let him glorify God" (1 Peter 4:16).

4. *Be selective when employing the aid of worldly powers.* After Paul's arrest in Jerusalem, we read in Acts 23 that over 40 of the Jews took an oath to ambush and kill him. Paul's nephew overheard some discussion of the plot and warned Paul. At that point Paul made a decision to inform the tribune who was holding him for trial. That might have been comparable to calling the police.

The tribune assigned hundreds of soldiers to whisk Paul out of the city that night and accompany him to Antipatris, some 40 miles away. The next day 70 of the horsemen continued on as Paul's bodyguard to deliver him safely to Governor Felix in Ceasarea. The cause for such extraordinary precautions against Paul's assassination may have been his Roman citizenship and the fact that during his inquest the tribune had abused Paul's rights before he knew of Paul's citizenship.

Did Paul know that he was engaging a small army when he notified the tribune? We don't know. Was he sure that the tribune's actions would not harm anyone? We don't know that either. Things turned out well, and Paul was sent on his way to Rome as the Lord had revealed to him (Acts 23:11). But as with occasions when we call the police, things could have become violent.

On an earlier occasion Jesus decided against trusting the

society in which He was living: "Now when he was in Jerusalem at the Passover feast, many believed in his name when they saw the signs which he did; but Jesus did not trust himself to them, because he ... knew what was in man" (John 2:23-25). Maybe more to the point was Rahab who hid the Hebrew spies from the Jericho police. Her life was not only spared for it, but she became acclaimed for her faith.

Jesus said, "Behold, I send you out as sheep in the midst of wolves; so be wise as serpents and innocent as doves. Beware of men ..." (Matthew 10:16, 17). This counsel should guide our use of the forces of this world's system. When we can do so without betraying the kingdom of our Lord, fine. But we must remember the character of our Kingdom, and even now we must "live as in the day."

What are the ethics of the kingdom of the day? "Do not resist one who is evil. But if any one strikes you on the right cheek, turn to him the other also; and if any one would sue you and take your coat, let him have your cloak as well; and if any one forces you to go one mile, go with him two miles. Give to him who begs from you, and do not refuse him who would borrow from you. You have heard that it was said, 'You shall love your neighbor and hate your enemy.' But I say to you, Love your enemies and pray for those who persecute you, so that you may be sons of your Father who is in heaven" (Matthew 5:39-45).

Dave Jackson, born and raised on the West Coast, received his initial Christian training in an evangelical tradition which fostered a deep desire to love and serve the Lord and other people. This background later found much of its fulfillment in the context of intentional Christian communities where he and his family have lived for eleven years. His earlier books, *Living Together in a World Falling Apart*, written with his wife, Neta (1974), and *Coming Together* (1978), dealt extensively with life in community.

Jackson received a BA in journalism from Judson College and graduated from Multnomah School of the Bible. He has worked as an editor with David C. Cook Publishing Co., *Campus Life* Magazine, and on a series of technical textbooks published in 1975 by John Wiley and Sons. He has also been a free-lance contributor to numerous Christian magazines.

The ethical turmoil of dealing with crime and violence was magnified for Jackson in 1968 when he was called to riot duty with the Army National Guard following the assassination of Martin Luther King, Jr. He was assigned to patrol the area around his Chicago storefront church, brandishing his weapons before people he loved—some of whom were brothers and sisters in Christ. Similarly, at the '68 Democratic Convention in Chicago his military duties conflicted with his role as a messenger of Christ's love.

These and other experiences uniquely equip Jackson to report and reflect upon the urban crime and violence experienced by Reba Place Fellowship in Evanston, Illinois, where he is one of the pastoral elders. The Jacksons and their son Julian (11) and daughter Rachel (5) have been members of this church community since 1973.